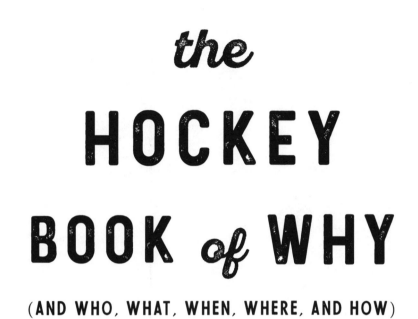

the
HOCKEY
BOOK *of* WHY
(AND WHO, WHAT, WHEN, WHERE, AND HOW)

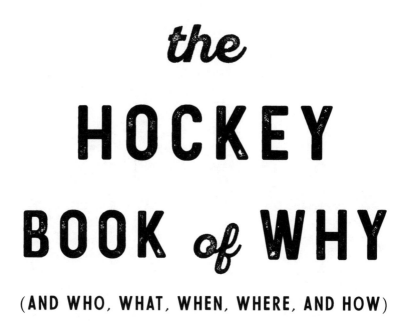

the
HOCKEY
BOOK *of* WHY

(AND WHO, WHAT, WHEN, WHERE, AND HOW)

THE ANSWERS TO QUESTIONS
YOU'VE ALWAYS WONDERED
ABOUT THE FASTEST GAME ON ICE

MARTIN GITLIN

LYONS
PRESS

Essex, Connecticut

An imprint of Globe Pequot, the trade division of
The Rowman & Littlefield Publishing Group, Inc.
4501 Forbes Blvd., Ste. 200
Lanham, MD 20706
www.rowman.com

Distributed by NATIONAL BOOK NETWORK

British Library Cataloguing in Publication Information available

Library of Congress Cataloging-in-Publication Data

Name: Gitlin, Marty author.
Title: The hockey book of why (and who, what, when, where, and how) : the
    answers to questions you've always wondered about the fastest game on
    ice / Martin Gitlin.
Description: Essex, Connecticut : Lyons Press, [2023] | Includes
    bibliographical references. | Summary: "This book provides a slew of
    questions and in-depth answers concerning the traditions, rules,
    records, and history of hockey. From the early days of the sport to the
    hugely popular game seen today, Martin Gitlin answers questions even the
    most knowledgeable fan may have pondered"– Provided by publisher.
Identifiers: LCCN 2023004826 (print) | LCCN 2023004827 (ebook) | ISBN
    9781493070923 (trade paperback) | ISBN 9781493070930 (epub)
Subjects: LCSH: Hockey–Miscellanea. | Hockey–Anecdotes. |
    Hockey–Records.
Classification: LCC GV847 .G55 2023 (print) | LCC GV847 (ebook) | DDC
    796.96202–dc23/eng/20230203
LC record available at https://lccn.loc.gov/2023004826
LC ebook record available at https://lccn.loc.gov/2023004827

Introduction

Inclusion among what are considered the major sports in the United States has for decades seemed a bit fuzzy. Football, baseball, and basketball remain no-brainers. Their respective levels of popularity among fans and media coverage make them obvious choices.

But what about hockey? Enough support certainly exists in most American cities with National Hockey League (NHL) franchises to make an argument that it belongs on that list. Yet even in those towns, some believe the sport is embraced only by a hardcore base and that interest is not widespread. True or not, perception can often be interpreted as reality. Such is also perceived about folks living in areas without teams. They seemingly give far more attention to the National Football League (NFL), National Basketball Association (NBA), and Major League Baseball (MLB) than they give to hockey.

Why? The answer to that question motivated the creation of *The Hockey Book of Why (and Who, What, When, Where, and How)*. It is greatly due to a lack of knowledge about the sport beyond the southern border of Canada, where it is the national pastime and the home of fanatical fans east, west, north, and south. A majority of Americans do not understand the rules, traditions, and history of hockey at the NHL or international levels.

The complexities of the sport itself play a role in those misunderstandings or lack of relevance. Millions simply do not know the game well enough to enjoy it beyond a short glimpse of action on TV. But their fandom might rise along with their levels of expertise.

First come the basics. How was hockey born? What are some of the guidelines under which the sport is played? Which teams have historically dominated NHL and Olympic competitions? Once that understanding is established, a potential fan will thirst for a more nuanced and deeper knowledge. How has the puck evolved over the years? When did women's hockey become an Olympic sport? What NHL defenseman revolutionized the game as a prolific scorer?

It's all here. *The Hockey Book of Why (and Who, What, When, Where, and How)* is intended to cover every angle and expand both understanding of and appreciation for the sport. It is also meant to enjoy. So, take a fun slide down the ice and learn a bit of everything about a game whose roots some believe can be traced back more than two centuries.

QUESTION 1: HOW WAS ICE HOCKEY INVENTED?

Welcome to the unknown. Any time it can be legitimately claimed that the roots of a sport extend back four thousand years, you know that history is a bit murky.

Nailing down even the century in which hockey was born is impossible. But records exist of a ball-and-stick game being played by folks in China, Persia, or Egypt around 2000 BCE. Archaeologists have even found evidence of such a sport in Greece three thousand years earlier.

Forms of hockey were most certainly enjoyed by native North Americans well before the arrival of Viking explorers and other Europeans that followed in the late 1400s and beyond. Those who arrived noted native people playing a game that can be considered a precursor to lacrosse but that looked a bit like hockey as well. Some museums even display proof that the Aztecs embraced such activity.

Even the derivation of the name "hockey" has been debated. Some have asserted it comes from the French *hoquet*, which can be translated into "shepherd's stave," with the second word meaning a wooden post or plank that presumably represented the sides of a goal. But others claim the name comes from cork bangs, called stoppers, that were used as the original pucks instead of wooden balls. The cork bangs came from barrels containing German hock ale, also known as "hocky." Accurate or not, it is one interesting explanation.[1]

Even the dates and circumstances surrounding the launching of the contemporary game are tough to nail down. Canadians who are proud of their country's link to its national pastime have claimed that it was first played there, but a preponderance of evidence shows that the United Kingdom—not exactly a hockey hotbed today—was the birthplace of the modern sport. Research reveals its beginnings in the 1790s in Great Britain. Those same investigations indicate that the "hock ale" link to the word "hockey" was first made there rather than in North America.

Most surprising is the contention that such historical luminaries as scientist and evolution theorist Charles Darwin and King Edward VII were among the first hockey players. The following letter dated from Darwin to his son William, dated March 1, 1853, was discovered by historians and referenced games in which he participated in Shrewsbury, England, in the 1820s.

> My Dear Old Willy . . . have you got a pretty good pond to skate on? I used to be very fond of playing at Hocky on the ice in skates.[2]

The game was indeed known as "hocky" in nineteenth-century Britain. But that was not its original name. It had been referred to as hurley, hurling, bandy, shinty, and shinny. And the modern game has even been traced back to seventeenth-century Scotland, though more than a century later, one news story from Glasgow reported that two teenage boys were playing "shinty" on thin ice in 1803 when they fell through and did not survive.

The earliest Scottish reference to what they called the game of "chamiare" occurs in the following passage from roughly 1607 in *The Historie of the Kirk of Scotland*, which was published in 1646: "The sea freized so farre as it ebbed, and sindrie went in to shippes upon yee, and played at the chamiare a mile within the sea marke."[3]

European claims to the invention of the contemporary sport were even legitimized in a painting believed to be by Benedictus Antonio van Assen that shows young Londoners playing the game with sticks on ice around December 1796 during a cold snap in that city. And a book about the Great Irish Famine of 1847 by John O'Rourke cited "teams of gentlemen [playing a] match of hurling on the ice of the River Shannon near Portumna."[4]

So, what was Canada's contribution to the founding of ice hockey? That too can be debated. Some believe the sport was invented in Nova Scotia. The Ministry of Transport in that province was even convinced to place a sign on the highway claiming that it was the birthplace of hockey. Canada has also reasonably laid claim to the first organized indoor hockey game, which was played in Montreal on March 3, 1875.

That battle was waged at the Victoria Skating Rink based on rules set forth by McGill University students, some of whom participated in the event. Most involved in establishing those guidelines was eventual McGill law student James G. A. Creighton. One major change was the use of a wooden disk, eventually known as a "puck," rather than a lacrosse ball. The match, which was promoted by the *Montreal Gazette*, featured two nine-men teams, one of which Creighton captained. The comparatively small rosters reflected the littler rink used in the indoor game as opposed to the outdoor variety. Hockey played on large frozen ponds or rivers involved as many players as could compete comfortably. The number of players for indoor hockey was lowered to seven at the Montreal Winter Carnival Tournament in the 1880s.

The following excerpt from an article published in the *Gazette* the day after the first organized hockey game lauded the uniqueness and safety of the budding sport.

> At the Rink last night a very large audience gathered to witness a novel contest on the ice. The game of hockey, though much in vogue on the ice in New England and other parts of the United States, is not much known here, and in consequence the game of

last evening was looked forward to with great interest. Hockey is played usually with a call, but last night, in order that no accident should happen, a flat block of wood was used, so that it should slide along the ice without rising, and thus going among the spectators to their discomfort. The game is like Lacrosse in one sense—the block having to go through flats placed around 8 feet apart in the same manner as the rubber ball—but in the main the old country game of shinty gives the best idea of hockey.[5]

Though the *Gazette* referenced ice hockey in America, it is clear that the indoor game had arrived. It now featured a flat wooden block to clobber with sticks and fewer players competing on the ice. And that Canada played a significant role in the creation and popularity of what is recognized as the modern sport is undeniable.

QUESTION 2: WHO INSPIRED THE NAME OF THE STANLEY CUP?

There is no more famous, coveted, and inspiring trophy in North American team sports than the Stanley Cup. Its allure is considered downright mystical. First awarded in 1893, it is still annually held aloft and paraded around the ice by the NHL champions immediately after capture by a finals victory. The Stanley Cup is not only a trophy but also the name of the competition during which teams battle to win it. But many fans and players have limited or even no knowledge about the history of the glorious reward itself.

The Stanley Cup was worth $50 when first manufactured in 1892. It is now priceless. Its original purchaser was Canadian Sir Frederick Arthur Stanley, Lord Stanley of Preston and son of the Fourteenth Earl of Derby. His motivation was to present it annually to his country's championship team as a reminder of his time as its governor general.

The historically appropriate bunch that earned the initial reward was the Montreal Amateur Athletic Association, whose Montreal Hockey Club won the Amateur Hockey Association of Canada in 1893 (there were no playoffs).[6]

That Cup certainly bore no resemblance to the one glorified today. It was a bowl that stood barely seven inches high and less than a foot wide. The modern trophy honors that one. A similar bowl rests now atop the modern Stanley Cup, which boasts a full height of 35.25 inches and weighs 37 pounds.[7]

Eventual NHL founder J. L. Gibson was merely a toddler when the first Cup was presented. It was given annually from 1893 to 1906 to the winner of a series of games featuring amateur teams throughout Canada. But the sport was changing. In 1907, the Montreal Wanderers declared themselves professional and snagged Stanley by outscoring the New Glasgow Cubs 17–3 in a two-match rout. By that time, several amateur clubs had begun sprinkling in professional players.[8]

The first season of the professional National Hockey Association (NHA) in 1910 gave the Stanley Cup a steadier home. The league snagged possession of the trophy while battling teams in the Pacific Coast Hockey Association and eventually teams based in the United States. A series of interleague clashes for supremacy determined which earned the award that was becoming more celebrated every year.

American clubs indeed made their talents known. The Pacific Coast Hockey Association's Portland Rosebuds nearly upset the Montreal Canadiens in 1916. Then, that league's Seattle Metropolitans defeated Montreal the following year.

The NHL did not exactly explode into existence in 1917. It housed just three teams—Ottawa, Montreal, and Toronto—playing an eighteen-game schedule. But it dominated Stanley Cup competition against other league champions for nearly a decade before the trophy became the sole province of the NHL. The lone exception was the Victoria Cougars of the Western Canada Hockey League, which defeated Hamilton to take the Cup in 1925.

By that time, the NHL boasted six teams, including the Boston Bruins as the first American entry. That league gained sole ownership of the Cup by 1927 despite disputes from other leagues. Its standing as the private domain of the most prized trophy in North American team sports was solidified twenty years later, when it entered an agreement with the Cup's trustees to reject such challenges.

By that time, the Stanley Cup had undergone a face-lift. The simple bowl had been transformed into a three-foot-high trophy. The extra space had become necessary when, in 1924, a fateful decision to allow the inscription of the names of players on championship teams every year. Bands were added below the bowl to create room for those signatures.

A series of changes had been launched. In 1939, it was revamped into a thinner cigar-shaped trophy. Nearly a decade later it was transformed into a two-piece style with a wide barrel-shaped base and removable bowl and collar. The more familiar form featuring a ceremonial bowl sitting atop three tiered bands, collar, and five uniform bands at the base was introduced in 1958.[9]

NHL president Clarence Campbell became worried in 1963. He felt the Stanley Cup was too brittle to be carried about by players who had earned the annual crown. So, he ordered that a presentation trophy be created for that purpose to keep the priceless one safe. A replica of the legendary trophy was built in 1993 and remains in the Hockey Hall of Fame when the presentation Cup is on the road.

The Stanley Cup remains the lone trophy in professional sports that features the inscriptions of every winning-team participant. That has resulted in several signatures giving it a sense of uniqueness. Among them is that of World War II–era Toronto Maple Leafs goaltender Turk Broda, who signed it both "Turk" and "Walter," his given name. Montreal goaltender Jacques Plante signed the Stanley Cup five times and used a different name on each occasion. The 1971–1972 Boston Bruins are listed on the trophy as the "BQSTQN BRUINS."

One could hardly imagine athletes in any other sport parading around their championship trophy throughout the field or court or diamond nor taking it on the road with them. Nor could anyone envision stars of the game placing signatures on the ultimate prizes they earned. It is what makes the Stanley Cup the most hallowed trophy of them all.[10]

QUESTION 3: HOW HAS THE PUCK EVOLVED OVER THE YEARS?

The earliest images of ice hockey featured players slapping a wooden slab or even a ball with a stick. One could hardly imagine the modern game using such archaic equipment. The game did not begin to fly to its current heights until a sturdier and more reliable centerpiece was created.

First, a bit of terminology—though the roots of the word "puck" remain a bit cloudy, many believe it originated from the Irish word "poke" that extends back to the game of hurling. The current spelling became accepted in Canada in the late 1860s after use in an article about the sport published in Montreal.

Though never established as truth, it has been offered that the first puck was made by cutting a black rubber ball in half or slicing off the rounded edges to stop it from bouncing. The earliest pucks were manufactured with wood or rubber. It has even been asserted that in the late nineteenth century some hockey aficionados slammed sticks into frozen cow dung to play the sport.[11]

Thus began the quest for the perfect hockey puck. In the early 1900s, they were made by gluing together two pieces of rubber. There was one major problem: They often split apart during games. So beveled edges were introduced around 1931. That too proved unsatisfactory.

What is considered the modern puck design began about a decade later. It is a solid, flat black disc three inches in diameter and one inch thick made of vulcanized rubber. Pucks are manufactured in several countries, including Canada, Slovakia, Russia, China, and the Czech Republic. The NHL, however, is supplied only by the Quebec company InGlasCo, the largest puck manufacturer in the world.

Professional leagues such as the NHL freeze their pucks during games to prevent them from bouncing and sticking to the ice. Its side is embedded with dozens of tiny, textured, raised grooves that allow sticks to grip them when they are being handled and shot.[12]

Regulation NHL pucks are manufactured by hand through a mix of granular rubber, bonding material, antioxidants, and coal dust. That concoction is placed in a two-part mold compressed at room temperature. The rubber is shaped into circular logs three inches wide and then cut into one-inch pieces before hardening. Each piece of rubber is placed into a mold the exact size of a puck and compressed. Logos silk-screened into the puck add the final touch. They are then examined to ensure proper size and weight.

There was one problem both for fans at arenas and those watching on television. The puck was too small to be followed closely, particularly when flying through the air or on the ice one hundred miles per hour on a slapshot. The NHL determined that the issue played a role in low TV ratings and a lack of popularity in comparison to other major sports, especially among potential American fans. So, the league and Fox Sports Network tried something new in 1996. They placed a tiny battery and computer board into its pucks, as well as holes so it could communicate with infrared emitters with sensor devices inside the arena. That created a glowing blue halo effect and red or green trail on the screen when players shot or passed the puck. Fox introduced the new technology with great fanfare. One voiceover proclaimed to fans that they would "witness the biggest technological breakthrough in the history of sport."[13]

Dedicated hockey fans did not take kindly to what Fox crowed as a remarkable achievement. Yahoo Sports hockey writer Greg Wychynski described that horror in a way that American fans could understand: with a reference to football. "Imagine if you were watching the Super Bowl and every time the running back disappeared in a pile of tacklers he started glowing like a blueberry from Chernobyl." An ESPN reader poll in 2002 chose the innovation as the sixth worst in sports history, though one must question the voters, who placed free agency as the number one choice. But *Huffington Post* writer Evan Winiker deemed the glowing puck as "the worst sports broadcasting innovation of our time."[14]

The NHL tampered again with the puck for its own purposes starting in 2019. The league added sensors to the discs, as well as cameras and antennae high above the ice surface, to track and analyze their movements during games.

Pucks aside from those manufactured for the NHL feature variations. Among the examples are blue, four-ounce varieties made for children and ten-ounce discs for adults wishing to develop their shots. Two-pound pucks are even created for those on strength-training regimens.[15]

QUESTION 4: WHY IS FIGHTING MORE ACCEPTED IN HOCKEY THAN IN OTHER SPORTS?

The date was March 3, 1875. The venue was the Victoria Skating Rink in Montreal. The combatants—both literally and figuratively—had concluded activities that extended beyond participating in the first organized indoor hockey game. Play on the ice was followed by a melee among players, spectators, and those waiting to use the arena for skating.[16]

The melee was certainly not the first in the history of hockey. The physical nature of the game had forever lent itself to bad blood and battles. But it also emerged as a way to police the sport and prevent brawls involving more than those originally involved from breaking out.

It has been speculated that the seeds of fighting in hockey were planted in Europe by those who had watched native Canadians play a bruising brand of lacrosse. Among the attractions for fans of the new sport of hockey was watching fights. And settling scores on the ice allowed teams and players to avoid getting the authorities involved.[17]

Such tactics did not deter critics from decrying violence in hockey that extended beyond hard checking and aggressive stick handling and carried over beyond the playing of the game. But fighting and reactions to it are nearly as old as the sport itself. Among the first examples occurred in 1890 during a barnstorming tour of the Rideau Hall Rebels, which competed out of Ottawa. That club was playing the Granite Hockey Club in Toronto when a brawl broke out that alarmed hockey officials.

Soon thereafter, Rideau member Arthur Stanley (son of Stanley Cup founder Lort Stanley Preston) met with others to create a new league with the specific intent of halting such lawlessness on the ice. "Part of that meeting was to prevent the activities that happened in Toronto from happening again," said Kevin Slater of the Society for International Hockey Research. "Specifically, they didn't like getting their asses kicked."[18]

Regulations adopted by the newly formed Ottawa Hockey Association did little to curb fisticuffs that often led to bloodshed. Neither did the creation of the National Hockey League in 1917. So, five years later that organization implemented Rule 56, which mandated a five-minute major penalty for fighting.

The impact of that policy proved minimal. After all, the only result was that one player from each team landed in the penalty box, thereby keeping personnel on the ice at an even level. Fighting remained an accepted and even necessary, according to some, part of the NHL.

Until the 1970s, however, it was considered a separate activity from the game itself with no influence on outcome. It was in that decade that teams such as the Philadelphia Flyers—otherwise known as the Broad Street Bullies—and the Big Bad Bruins of Boston began using fighting as an intimidation tactic that indeed played a role in their successes. They featured bruising players whose sole purpose was that of an enforcer. And it worked—the Flyers won two consecutive Stanley Cup championships.

Fighting as a method of intimidation and the practice itself lessened in recent years while the NHL had taken steps to reduce the number of violent incidents by instituting two-minute penalties for removing one's helmet before throwing down. But one must understand that fighting still serves several purposes in hockey.

Among them is protection of the goaltender, who spends their evening trying to stop pucks flying in at one hundred miles per hour and whose importance to the success or failure of a team is immeasurable. It is believed that teammates must disallow opponents from running into their goaltenders or jabbing them with their sticks.

Unwritten rules also mandate that enforcers must protect premier offensive talent. Players who create offense and can score are so valuable in a game often won with two or three goals that they too must be protected from opponents deemed willing and able to bend the rules to stop them. Creative offensive players must be given the space to skate, pass, and shoot.

Another purpose of fighting—or at least the threat of it—is to gain a psychological advantage over an opponent. Teams that play each other many times during the season and often meet in the playoffs cannot allow themselves to be intimidated by that foe. Fighting has played a role in nurturing some of the greatest rivalries in the history of the NHL and, to a lesser extent, the international game.

Fighting can also save careers. Some enforcers have admitted that they did not enjoy that role but understood that such expectations of them on the ice provided them a purpose that kept them employed. Most hockey fans, however, feel that some who fight only because of a penchant for bullying and enjoy instigating brawls do not belong on the ice.

Several factors beyond rule enforcement have resulted in a shrinking number of fights in the NHL since peaking in the early 2000s. One is player unity, which has strengthened over the years. The league has also encouraged clean play. During the 2018–2019 season, it had fewer than two hundred games with a fighting major, which marked a first in the modern era. And the goons were gone. The era of the enforcer had long since ended. Teams required all their players to boast skills that helped them win.[19]

Fighting will likely never fade out of hockey completely. But only a sadistic few yearn to see a return to the days in which many games were marred by brawls.

QUESTION 5: WHEN DID GOALIES BEGIN WEARING MASKS?

One might assume the advent of the goalie mask is nearly as old as the sport itself. It figures that some goaltender got whomped in the head by a flying disc in the late nineteenth century or early twentieth century and decided he needed protection in the future.

Well, one would assume wrong. Not only did no man don a mask while minding a net until 1927. But the first player to put safety first in this way was a woman. Her name was Elizabeth Graham. And she was trying to stop shots for Queen's University.[20]

It all seems ridiculous in the modern era with NHL Skills competition winners slapping pucks as fast as 102.8 miles per hour. But masks were unheard of in organized hockey for more than a half-century.

The first man to decide he wanted to make sure he kept all his teeth was Montreal Maroons goaltender Clint Benedict on February 20, 1930. His use of the leather covering was motivated by a shattered cheekbone. And his arrival on the ice that day for a battle with the New York Americans inspired a mocking newspaper account that read, "Clint looked like as if he had stepped out of the Dumas novel, 'The Iron Mask,' or in the modern manner, was appearing as a visitor from Mars."[21]

The Hockey Hall of Famer had gained greater fame four years earlier for pitching three consecutive shutouts for the Maroons in the finals against the Victoria Cougars. And he had deemed wearing a mask a necessity after a puck struck by Canadiens center Howie Morenz hit him in the face a month earlier and knocked him unconscious. Benedict remained hospitalized for a month with cheekbone and nose injuries that negatively affected his vision. He returned to the ice six weeks later with the crude mask, but then discarded it a few games later because he could not see well past the thick nosepiece. Ironically and tragically, his career ended after another Morenz slapshot nailed him in the throat.

Even then the mask did not catch on. That one did not even cover his entire face. The first to wear one that did was Japan's Teiji Honma during the 1936 Winter Olympics (which was shamefully allowed to be hosted by Adolf Hitler in Nazi Germany).

What seems like an obviously necessary protection today remained ignored for more than two decades thereafter. Legend Jacques Plante of the Canadiens emerged as the next goaltender to don a mask, and he too was motivated by an existing injury. He had been drilled in the face by a puck slapped by Andy Bathgate during a 1959 game against the New York Rangers and returned to the net later wearing a fiberglass covering that inspired cat-calls from fans and coaches. Montreal coach Toe Blake at first disallowed Plante from entering the game wearing the mask, but Plante refused to enter without it. That forced Blake to relent.[22] And nobody was laughing when Plante led the Canadiens on an eighteen-game winning streak.[23]

The snug fit of the fiberglass mask resulted in greater comfort. Soon, other NHL goaltenders began following suit, and a trend was born. A decade later most goalies wore masks. There were few holdouts by 1970. The last to remain unprotected was Andy Brown of the Pittsburgh Penguins in 1974.

By that time, an aggressive evolution of the hockey mask had begun to add greater comfort and protection. Companies competing to gain business in the NHL and international games added padding and experimented with new styles. FibroSport discovered one innovation still used today by adding ridges to the forehead of the mask to ensure structural firmness. Mask manufacturers in the 1970s experimented with a wire cage that fit in front of the fiberglass shell. That marked the beginning of the modern combo style mask that combines both. It allows the cage to absorb impact and disperse it to the outer edges of the mask rather than the goaltender's head. Eventually more padding was added, which provided even greater protection.

In 1972, Boston Bruins goalie Gerry Cheevers had his trainer paint stitches on his fiberglass mask whenever a puck struck him in the head, thereby becoming the first to feature a design. It became what some consider the most famous face covering in hockey history, and Cheevers has been recognized as a pioneer in mask art and design.[24]

By the 1990s, the combination style masks were supplemented with materials such as carbon and aramid fiber that were layered between the fiberglass for more durability and resistance. The Profile model created by mask designer Jerry Wright early that decade resulted in a sleeker look with chiseled lines most commonly worn by modern goaltenders.[25]

By the 2020s, goalies were using their masks as a means of personal expression. Intricate designs made each one unique. Some featured drawings that celebrated team nicknames. Others showed the love of pop culture icons. Still others featured designs that expressed fondness of family members or friends who had passed away or played positive roles in their lives.

Masks of the modern era don't just protect goaltenders from pucks flying toward their noggins. They add color and personality to a sport that seeks to turn casual fans into passionate ones and spark the interest of those yet to turn on to hockey. Perhaps the evolution is not complete, but the mask has come a long way since a young female netminder decided to wear one nearly a century ago.

QUESTION 6: WHY IS HOCKEY MORE POPULAR IN CANADA THAN IN THE UNITED STATES?

One common belief is that the oversaturation of popular sports in the United States leaves little room for hockey to gain traction among most US sports fans. There is some truth to that. But the reasons that the game has been forever linked far more to Canada than the United States are many.

Among them is history. The first organized indoor game was played in Montreal. The NHL was born in 1917 with four Canadian teams—the Boston Bruins became the first US franchise in 1924. By that time, baseball had long been recognized as the national pastime and many other factors had become established for a lack of passion for hockey in the United States.

Its popularity grew among Americans but not with the same rapidity and fervor as it did in the nation up north as time marched on. Youth hockey organizations sprung up throughout Canada as the game became embraced. That was seen as natural for a cold-weather sport. It is why kids from cities such as Buffalo and Detroit also began playing in earnest but not those in southern states.

Canada has been considered a hotbed for young prospects since the birth of organized hockey. Meanwhile, the youth of the United States joined hot stove baseball leagues and dabbled more in a wide range of sports such as basketball, football, and, eventually, soccer. Hockey was viewed as an expensive undertaking that cost hundreds, even thousands, of dollars in equipment and travel. It was no wonder that in the late 1960s only about 2 percent of all NHL players were American, even though four of the six teams were based in the United States. About 25 percent of all NHL players in 2019 had been born in the United States, but that still lagged far behind the number from Canada.

Though youth hockey has certainly grown in the United States over the years, the differences have remained stark. The number of registered American players in 2019 totaled 567,908, nearly 50,000 fewer than in Canada. Given that the United States boasts a population nine times greater than its neighbors, that is a huge gap.[26]

Many hockey heroes from the past and modern days who have been beloved by Canadians go unrecognized by American fans. Names of other sports stars drip off the tongues of the latter. The legends of hockey past and present don't register in comparison to Babe Ruth or Michael Jordan or Tom Brady.

That hockey is vastly more popular in Canada and will likely always be is a given for a myriad of reasons. Most US cities that boast an NHL franchise attract hardcore fans to arenas. The top eleven teams in attendance during the 2021–2022 season were all based in the United States. And Ottawa placed last. But some have argued that the percentage of moderate hockey fans is far higher in Canada, where most folks have at least some interest in the sport. That distinction in the United States skews more to the other three major sports. And there is little hockey interest in cities outside the NHL realm. Polls have revealed that fewer than 5 percent of people in the United States consider hockey their favorite sport. Some have claimed that soccer has bypassed hockey in the hearts and minds of US sports fans.[27]

Television ratings speak volumes. One example was the 2021 Stanley Cup finals, which attracted 70 percent of all potential viewers in Canada but well under three million per game in the United States.[28]

Hockey aficionados who would like to add more to their ranks have been studying that discrepancy for decades. Though it extends far beyond an inability or at least unwillingness to learn and understand the sport and follow the action on TV, those certainly remain prime factors. Many Americans who have turned on to hockey have become lifelong fans. But the vast majority feel they have neither the time nor inclination. The game is a tough watch on the tube. The puck is difficult to follow and the players nearly impossible to identify moving nonstop on the screen.

This becomes a chicken-egg issue. Does a lack of television coverage beyond the Stanley Cup reflect weak interest in hockey in the United States or has it caused the weak interest? The NHL is virtually ignored by the major networks (cable and otherwise), who have vacillated between signing contracts with the league for a "Game of the Week" format or bypassing the sport completely.

The game has another problem among American fans that ties in with poor TV ratings, though it's not as pronounced as it is with soccer. And that is a lack of scoring. It is one reason football and basketball have, in most polls, emerged as the two most popular sports in the United States. US viewers—particularly those with weak attention spans—crave the constant action that hockey provides. But they also like high point totals inherently unable to be achieved in sports such as hockey, baseball, and soccer.

Some believed hockey would begin to flourish in the United States beyond 1980, when a group of plucky college kids during the Cold War stunned the polished Russians in the semifinals of the Winter Olympics in what many still consider the greatest upset in the history of international sports competition. Eventually, the NHL opened up to European talent and expansion continued to place more teams in US cities, but the interest in hockey that had been piqued after the US team won the gold medal was short-lived.

One reason is a lack of diversity in hockey. Though the number of Black American players in the NHL has grown in recent years, it still can't hold a candle to representation in the other major sports, even baseball, which also boasts a huge percentage of Hispanic players. The result is a distinct lack of minority viewership and fandom inside arenas. It is no wonder that the NBA and NFL, both of which feature majority Black player participation, are also by far the most popular sports in the United States among the minority population. Only 3.5 percent of the Canadian population is Black. The differences are stark.

The large number of reasons why hockey is embraced more in Canada than in the United States likely means that that will never change. For those who would like to see the gap shrink, the best they can hope for is that the NHL gains at least some interest among US fans. But the problems that persist sometimes seem impossible to overcome.

QUESTION 7: WHAT TEAMS MADE UP THE NHL'S ORIGINAL SIX?

Despite the greater popularity of hockey in Canada, only two franchises from that country competed among what became known as
the "Original Six." They were the Montreal Canadiens and Toronto
Maple Leafs. The others were the New York Rangers, Boston
Bruins, Detroit Red Wings, and Chicago Black Hawks, now known
as Blackhawks.

That setup was established in 1942 and remained intact until
the number increased to twelve in 1967. The NHL had been the
least aggressive major professional sports league in North America
regarding expansion. Though some considered the doubling of
franchises that year as reckless, it did stretch the boundaries to
the West Coast of the United States well after the NFL, NBA, and
MLB had done the same.

The league added the California Seals and Los Angeles Kings,
as well as the Minnesota North Stars, Philadelphia Flyers, Pittsburgh
Penguins, and St. Louis Blues. That another Canadian city such as
Vancouver was not awarded a club raised both eyebrows and ire.
The Canucks did not arrive until 1970 when the Buffalo Sabres
were added as well.

An eye on America had been obvious for decades before
the Original Six. The NHL, which had been born as a result of
the National Hockey Association (NHA) going defunct, boasted
only Canadian teams in its first seven seasons, including two in
Montreal (Canadiens and Maroons). The Bruins were added in
1924, then the Pittsburgh Pirates and New York Americans the

following year. The NHL continued to expand. Teams were placed in Detroit, Chicago, and Ottawa in 1927.

Soon, the Great Depression took a toll. The Philadelphia Quakers, St. Louis Eagles, and Montreal Maroons collapsed when they did not attract enough fans to handle operating expenses and dropped out. World War II also played a role in the construction of the Original Six. The Brooklyn Americans failed to survive due to not only financial issues but also the departure of players to fight overseas. The result of all those struggles was significant contraction. The NHL dropped from ten teams to six in 1942.[29]

And there it remained for a quarter-century. The NHL steadfastly rejected inquiries from other cities, including Cleveland, whose minor-league Barons had been a tremendous competitive and financial success. Owners simply did not want to share the wealth. But the overwhelming lure of a major television contract that would be offered if the league grew, especially along the West Coast, convinced one and all that expansion was beneficial.

But the established owners demanded one stipulation. They would have to remain in the same conference as the league split into two. All the new clubs—even Philadelphia and Pittsburgh—were placed (ridiculously from a geographic standpoint) in the West Division. The long-standing franchises yearned to maintain the strong rivalries and showed little interest in helping the newcomers competitively. But nobody was complaining.

"When they made expansion, they took the players that were expandable, put them on a team and called them a team," recalled Bob Kelly, who played for the new Flyers at the time. "We didn't have the real identity that an original six team has or the history behind that. [We were] just happy to be in the NHL."[30]

The result was tremendous imbalance. Every team in the West Division finished its first season with a losing record. Yet one had to emerge as a finalist. And that was St. Louis, which lost four more games than it won during the regular season yet battled the powerful Canadiens for the coveted Cup. The outcome was predictable. Montreal swept the series in four straight, though the plucky Blues lost each of them by just one goal.

Expansion in the hearts and minds of many brought the NHL out of the dark ages and placed them into conversation with the NFL, NBA, and MLB as a major sport. Interest surrounding such clubs as the 1970s Broad Street Bullies, otherwise known as the Philadelphia Flyers, justified a continued search for new franchises.

Additions continued at a rapid pace despite a lack of success in some cities. The New York Islanders and Atlanta Flames were added in 1972—but the Flames flamed out. The Washington Capitals and Kansas City Scouts joined in 1974, but the latter lasted only two seasons. The California Golden Seals bolted for Cleveland in 1976, but attendance and performance lagged and the franchise was moved to Minnesota. That club struggled and hightailed it to Dallas in 1983. The NHL welcomed four teams from the rival World Hockey Association in 1979, but three of them (Hartford, Quebec, and Winnipeg) left for greener pastures soon thereafter.

The furious comings and goings finally halted in the 1990s and beyond as additions no longer resulted in instability. Success was even gained where few believed hockey could thrive, as clubs such as the Dallas Stars, Tampa Bay Lightning, Carolina Hurricanes, and Nashville Predators soared toward the top of the league in attendance.

Yet the league remained to most neutral observers well behind the NFL, NBA, and MLB in popularity among Americans. Despite its aggressive attempts, the NHL has never been embraced by most in the United States beyond its most loyal and hardcore fans. A vexing and persisting problem attracting television viewers has continued for decades, resulting in a lack of name recognition for star players and overall weak interest in comparison to other sports.

QUESTION 8: WHAT ARE THE GREATEST RIVALRIES IN INTERNATIONAL HOCKEY?

Though rivalries abound at the Olympic and international levels, the majority of hockey aficionados believe Canada is involved in the most intense rivalries in both the men's and women's game.

Battles historically against the Russian men's team have catapulted that rivalry atop the list. But a comparatively new one against the United States quickly inspired some to declare it the most heated in women's hockey.

One might believe the Cold War played a role in the latter emerging as the most passionate rivalry in men's hockey. That was certainly true of the inspiring American upset of the Russians in the 1980 Olympic semifinal, but there have been few political ramifications permeating the competitions between Canada and the country known for decades as the Soviet Union. Rather, the greatness of their rivalry has been based mostly on their greatness in hockey and the epic games and series they have played against each other.

Canada was the first to establish itself as an on-ice super-power. Its team dominated the early Olympics, winning all four gold medals from 1920 to 1932 before falling in the finals to Great Britain in 1936, then winning it again in 1948 and 1952. Soon thereafter, the Russians joined the fray, participating in its first Winter Olympics in 1956 and immediately proving themselves as the best of the best, earning gold that year, as well as in 1964, 1968, 1972, and 1976. Only the shocker in 1980 interrupted the incredible run—they dominated the Olympics again in 1984 and

1988. The fall of the Soviet Union weakened its hockey teams, but Russia remained a threat and even managed a gold in 2018. Canada and Russia combined for seventeen Olympic championships—all but eight—through 2022. But many of their most memorable battles were waged in other competitions. The first among those and perhaps the most intense was the 1972 Summit Series.

Tensions over that event had been boiling since 1966, when the Canadian amateur champion Sherbrooke Beavers were invited behind the Iron Curtain to play the Central Red Army Sports Club. The Beavers expected to play their first game in Moscow but were dispatched by an unheated bus ninety-three miles to an outdoor rink in an army camp in Kalinin (now called Tver), where it was negative four degrees. The Russians destroyed the Beavers to the delight of the spectators, many of whom were soldiers brandishing assault rifles known as Kalashnikovs.

The more the Soviets scored, the angrier the Beavers became. They speared a Russian goaltender, which precipitated a brawl. Players were piled up on the ice punching and even yanking the ears of their rivals. With international relations in mind, Soviet coaches ordered they let the Canadians go. Soon the Beavers were invited to the Canadian Embassy, where an ambassador threatened to cancel the next two games if the players could not calm down and focus on hockey. Sherbrooke did just that and lost its final game against Moscow Spartak by just one goal.[31]

The ground rules had changed when the two nations faced off for the 1972 Summit Series in Moscow as the Canadians used their top professional players against the Russian Army team. The stronger competition was reflected in the scores, as both teams won three games. A three-goal blitz in the third period of the finale allowed Canada to forget the tie.

By that time, Canada and the Soviet Union were established as the premier hockey powers in the world both at the youth and adult levels. They competed in many memorable World Junior Championships and World Championships as well as Winter Olympics. The influx of Russian players into the NHL and the end of the Cold War certainly brought a higher level of civility to the rivalry that was achieved in 1966 while the rise of other countries on the ice eventually threatened their standing as the best on the planet. But it is undeniable that Russia vs. Canada remains historically the most heated international rivalry in the sport.

A much newer and far less political competition rose in the twenty-first century as the most intense in the women's game. And that was between the United States and Canada. While several other countries have rained on the parades of the Canadians and Russians in men's hockey, the American and Canadian women thoroughly dominated all other competition into the 2020s.

It would be impossible for either club to feel the same sense of history—women's hockey did not launch as a major competition until the 1990 International Ice Hockey Federation Championships. It did not become an Olympic sport until 1998. But the United States and Canada both proved so dominant over the next thirty years that their rivalry continued to gain momentum throughout that time. Only a defeat to Sweden in the 2006 Olympics halted the US momentum, while the Canadians were just once stymied in a loss to Finland in the 2019 World Championships. Canada won five Olympic gold medals to two for the United States and owned a 10–9 record in World Championship play.

The rivalry began in earnest at the 1998 Nagano Olympics, where the United States avenged several IHHF Championships losses to Canada by scoring six unanswered goals to win a round-robin game before beating its rival for the gold medal. The Canadians continued to rule other international competition heading into the 2002 Olympics in Salt Lake City. Both teams steamrolled into the finals before Canada avenged its 1998 defeat to take gold.

Canada earned the only shutout in head-to-head Olympic hockey against the United States to win the 2010 finals as goaltender Shannon Szabados stopped all twenty-eight shots headed her way. A pattern had begun to emerge. The United States reigned in World Championship play, while Canada dominated the Olympics. A new format allowed the two powers to compete more than once at the 2014 Sochi Olympics. And it provided the Canadians an opportunity to avenge defeat in the gold medal game, scoring with fifty-five seconds left in regulation and on a power play in overtime to again frustrate the US team.

The pattern continued. The United States won World Championships in 2015, 2016, and 2017, beating Canada twice along the way. But it needed to prove it could beat Canada on the biggest international stage—the 2018 Pyeongchang Games. And they did when Jocelyne Lamoureux-Davidson faked out Szabados in a shootout and scored, and then goaltender Maddie Rooney made one final stop to give the US team a 3–2 victory and their second gold. Canada took back gold in the 2022 finals after an overwhelming offensive display throughout the event by beating the United States by the same score.

It did not take that long for the players on both sides to embrace what they believed to be the most intense competition in international hockey. "I think the rivalry between Canada and the U.S. has been there since the inception," said Laura Schuler, who is the head coach of the Canadian team and played on the 1998 squad that lost to the Americans. "Every single time we've ever faced the U.S., it's been a one goal difference. It's gone into overtime. It's been a back-and-forth hockey game. It's best-on-best competition. I think that's what makes it so great."[32]

Rivalries shrink and grow in sports. Into the 2020s, the Canada-Russia men's rivalry appeared likely to stay the most intense on the international stage. But the Canada–United States women's battles seemed destined to remain the most heated in the world.

QUESTION 9: HOW MANY GOALIES HAVE SCORED A GOAL IN NHL HISTORY?

Among the rarest occurrences in hockey is a goal scored by a goaltender. It is even more rare than an unassisted triple play in major league baseball. Up through 2022, there were twelve instances of a goalie putting one into the opposite net (and fifteen unassisted triple plays).

Most unusual is that all twelve goaltender tallies have happened since 1979. They have generally scored directly and indirectly after opposing goaltenders have been pulled for an extra attacker in losing efforts.

Indirect goaltender goals are registered when they are the last to touch a puck on their own team before a player on the other side accidentally shoots it into the net. That was the circumstance surrounding New York Islanders netminder Billy Smith, who became the first to gain that distinction in 1979 during a game against the Colorado Rockies, who three years later moved to New Jersey to become the Devils. Smith turned away a shot that landed on the stick of Rob Ramage, whose errant pass slid down ice into the empty net. Since Smith was the last Islander to touch the puck, he was credited with the goal.

Philadelphia standout Ron Hextall became the first to directly shoot a puck into the net for a goal on December 8, 1987. He received a pass late in the game after the Bruins yanked Reggie Lemelin to gain an advantage two goals down. Hextall recognized a unique opportunity when it came his way. He sent the puck into the net. He must have liked the feeling—Hextall scored a playoff goal the next season against the Washington Capitals.

The most involved goaltender on both sides of the scoring fence was Hall of Famer Martin Brodeur, who turned back shots for the Devils at a prodigious rate. He joined Hextall on April 17, 1997, as a playoff scorer when he stopped a desperation slapper by the Canadiens behind his own net and sent a long shot that found its target to ensure a 5–2 victory. Two years later Ottawa goaltender Damian Rhodes was credited with a score as the last Senator to touch the puck. It counted against Brodeur, who had left the net on a delayed penalty and watched with consternation when teammates whiffed on a pass and the puck slid into the net.[33]

That incidence was sandwiched between two Brodeur goals, the second of which was earned on February 15, 2000, against Philadelphia. That too was a secondhand tally, but with far greater consequence. It proved to be the game-winner. And Brodeur was not done. The incredible length of his career allowed him to be credited with yet another goal in 2013 when his save careened onto the stick of a Flyer whose pass missed the mark and traveled into the unoccupied opposing net on a delayed penalty.

Not every goaltender tally was the result of pure luck. San Jose netminder Evgeni Nabokov displayed some talent with his team ahead by two goals against Vancouver on March 10, 2002. The Canucks were attempting to kill off a penalty in the waning seconds after pulling goalie Peter Skudra when the puck landed on Nabokov's skate. He noticed a crease of daylight down the ice and sent the disc softly between every skater into the open net. It marked the first power play goalie goal in league history.[34]

That was a particular rarity. Most such instances occurred when a player accidentally sends the puck into the goal after the opposing goaltender had been the last in his team to handle it. But with only twelve goalie goals in the books, they are all oddities—perhaps the rarest of the rate occurrences in major team sports.

QUESTION 10: WHAT IS A HAT TRICK, AND WHAT IS THE ORIGIN OF ITS NAME?

The "hat trick" is arguably the most well-known term in hockey. Even lukewarm fans of the sport know that it is used to honor the achievement of a player scoring three goals in one game. But the majority of those who can identify its meaning know nothing about its origin.

Hockey enthusiasts were certainly given an opportunity to tag a colorful name to that accomplishment, even on the first day of the inaugural NHL season. Four players tallied three or more goals on December 19, 1917. But Joe Malone of the Montreal Canadiens, Harry Hyland of the Montreal Wanderers, Cy Denneny of the Ottawa Senators, and Reg Noble of the Toronto Arenas received no more than a hearty congratulations and perhaps a beer or two purchased for them as a celebration.

But though the phrase "hat trick" had yet to be identified with hockey, it had existed for nearly six decades. It was used to describe the handiwork of British cricket bowler H. H. Stephenson, who was playing for an all-English squad against a team from South Yorkshire, when he took three consecutive wickets at the Hyde Park Grounds in Sheffield, meaning that he nailed the wooden stakes behind a batter three straight times. So impressive was the feat that a collection was taken up to buy a hat that was presented to Stephenson to honor the achievement.

How the term gained popularity in hockey has never been fully established. Some newspaper hockey writers began using it in the 1930s and 1940s. But other theories abound. Among them is one theory that traces the terms to a Guelph business known as

Biltmore Hats, which, according to the story, offered one hat in its collection to the highest-scoring players on its Mad Hatters junior team. Another assertion is that Montreal haberdashery Henri Henri offered a free hat to three-goal scorers at the legendary Forum in the 1950s.

The Hockey Hall of Fame has a different explanation. It claims the phrase was more specifically coined by Toronto hatter Sammy Taft, who promoted his business by offering a hat to any player who scored three goals in an NHL game played in that city. Taft billed himself as the world's most famous hatter and indeed sold about ten thousand head-toppers during the 1940s alone, including to such entertainment luminaries as Cab Calloway, Bob Hope, and Duke Ellington.[35]

According to legend, his store was visited in early 1946 by Chicago Black Hawks standout Alex Kaleta, who eyed a fedora but lacked the cash to pay for it. Always thinking about how to promote his business, Taft offered to give him the hat if he recorded at least three goals against the Maple Leafs that night. The added inspiration contributed to Kaleta scoring four of his team's five goals in a taut Toronto victory. Taft claimed to have heard of the achievement on the radio referred to as a "hat trick" and indeed presented the desired fedora to Kaleta.

Not one to trumpet individual accomplishments nor having any understanding of the possible importance to hockey lore of the gift he received, Kaleta gave his hat along with other clothing to youngest brother Arthur, who allowed it to disappear during a move in 1955. Arthur never realized the significance of the fedora until more than three decades after his older brother had died and Hockey Night in Canada aired a segment about the hat trick. "I was shocked," Arthur said. "If I had kept that hat, I'd be a millionaire. Actually, if I had kept that hat, it would be in the Hockey Hall of Fame where it belongs. But that was typical Alex. He was a terrific player but never put himself above anybody else and never said a word about the hat trick."[36]

The establishment and popularity of the "hat trick" inspired fans for generations to throw caps and hats onto the ice after a player scored his third goal in a game. That tradition originated in the 1970s but caused a dilemma for members of NHL organizations, who simply did not know what to do with the headwear once it landed on the playing surface. Some arenas gave them to the player who scored three goals to keep as mementos or given to charity. The Columbus Blue Jackets took a different approach. They collected all the hats from the first official hat trick registered in their home arena in 2001 and placed them on display.

The NHL once penalized home teams for what it considered a delay of game as hats flew from the stands onto the ice. But league officials recognized that it was merely a show of appreciation from fans to players and removed the penalty.[37]

An increase in goal scoring in more recent decades greatly increased the number of hat tricks in NHL competition. Wayne Gretzky, the most prolific goal scorer of all time, also boasted the most hat tricks through 2022 with fifty, including ten in the postseason. Explosive Mario Lemieux played in five hundred fewer games than Gretzky yet still managed to record forty hat tricks.[38]

The hat trick and fan reactions to it help give hockey its uniqueness among major team sports.

QUESTION 11: HOW DID THE TRADITION OF THROWN OCTOPUSES ON THE ICE BEGIN?

On October 29, 2009, Pete Cusimano died. His funeral was held in Sterling Heights, Michigan. He never played for the Detroit Red Wings, nor was he employed by the organization. He had simply run a fish shore for decades.[39]

But fans of the team, even those who never met Cusimano, felt like they knew him. They sensed a kinship with him. In 1952, he launched a tradition that became a staple of NHL games played in that city for generations. During the playoffs that year, he celebrated a Red Wings score by flinging an octopus onto the ice. His favorite team won that clash and completed a sweep of the Canadiens to snag the Stanley Cup.

Cusimano, perhaps as a promotion for his business or due to a superstitious nature, claimed that the sacrificial octopus influenced the outcome. After all, it had eight tentacles and that was the same number of playoff victories required at the time to win the NHL championship. For many years thereafter, he arrived at postseason battles armed with octopuses to toss onto the playoff surface after Detroit tallies.[40]

Fans followed suit. For years they maintained the tradition. The octopus became a legendary image in Detroit. One could be seen atop a downtown building, on buildings, and in gift shops. The Red Wings showed the slimy creatures on their video screen. Banners showing an octopus with a fierce grimace on its face, one tooth missing, and brandishing a hockey stick with one of its tentacles were placed on lampposts.

And it was all because of Cusimano, who was hanging with brother Jerry and talking hockey—their favorite subject—at the family fish market on that fateful April afternoon. While Pete was holding an octopus, Jerry came up with an idea. "Pete," he said, "if the Wings win eight straight games, they'll win the Cup. An octopus has eight legs. Let's take it to the game and throw it on the ice. It'll be good luck."[41]

The brothers Cusimano boiled the dead octopus to make it less gray and slimy and more maroon and rubbery, thereby preventing it from sticking to the ice. And they practiced throwing it to ensure maximum grip and distance. "If you try to throw it like a baseball, you'll throw your arm out," Pete explained years later. "I would fling it sidearm like a hand grenade. One time I missed and knocked a man's hat off. When he spotted what it was [that] hit him, he left and never came back to his seat . . . They don't smell too pretty, either."[42]

His heave in 1952 naturally came as a shock. It certainly took the referee by surprise. He skated toward the octopus and then did a double take. A Montreal player whacked it with a stick. Legend has it that the game announcer in the building was forced to warn spectators not to throw octopuses on the ice—as if that was a threat coming from anyone else.

Fans certainly did not heed the admonition for the future. The custom reached epic proportions at Joe Louis Arena decades later as the Red Wings embarked on their mini dynasty, winning two consecutive Stanley Cups in the late 1990s, then another in 2002. In one 1995 game, fans threw thirty-six octopuses on the ice, including one that weighed thirty-eight pounds. They showered the ice after Detroit goals and forced play to halt while they were removed and dumped into the Detroit River just outside the building. That rather unpleasant task was thrust upon operations manager Al Sabotka, whose efforts did not go unappreciated. The huge octopus lowered from the arena rafters amid a shower of dry ice before games was named Big Al.

Superstition involving other creatures real or unreal eventually permeated the hockey landscape. Florida Panther fans sought to inspire the players by tossing dozens of rubber plastic rats on the ice after they scored. The charges were indeed inspired—before one game, one Panther used a hockey stick to kill a rat in the locker room and the team went on to win. The rodent that gave its life was deemed a good luck charm.

That seemed fun and harmless enough. But the NHL was no longer laughing about the octopus. The league cracked down on the tradition due to game delays and cleanup hassles. The gunk that emanated from the octopuses when they landed on the ice worsened the task. During a 2009 playoff game at Joe Louis Arena, referees announced that the team would be assessed a delay-of-game penalty if one more slimy creature was tossed. Fans decided that the joy of flinging meant less to them than helping the Wings win. So the custom was reduced to a rarity.

Yet it was not destroyed. As a celebration to mark the last game played at Joe Louis Arena before the club moved its home games to Little Caesars Arena in 2017, patrons tossed thirty-five octopuses onto the playing surface. People for the Ethical Treatment of Animals (PETA) had begged two days earlier for folks to stop what the organization deemed cruel. "Octopuses are intelligent, sensitive animals who feel pain, and it's no more acceptable to kill one for such a disrespectful, frivolous, and stupid purpose than it is to throw dead bear cubs onto the ice during a Bruins game," said PETA president Ingrid Newkirk.[43]

The NHL might have cared less about the health of octopuses than it did about the distractions of flinging them on the ice. But the league was serious about putting a halt to the practice. When a Windsor man became the first to toss one at Little Caesars

Arena, he was booted out of the building and charged with a misdemeanor.[44]

By that time, fans of other hockey teams had put their own spin on the hurling of animals onto the ice. Among them was a Nashville Predators enthusiast who launched a skinned duck onto the playing surface during the 2017 Western Conference finals. During the Stanley Cup finals that year, a fan threw a catfish onto the ice and was escorted out of the arena.

One could never imagine such goings-on on the courts, diamonds, or fields of other major sports. But strange traditions have been embraced by hockey fans to a far greater extent. None have been more prevalent than octopus-flinging in the Motor City.

QUESTION 12: WHAT IS A FACEOFF AND WHEN DO THEY OCCUR?

Most hockey fans—even the lukewarm ones—can identify a faceoff. It happens when a referee drops the puck between the sticks of two opposing players who then battle for possession.

The difference in faceoff skills can prove crucial to the outcome. This is particularly true late in games when the winning team is trying to secure the puck to clear it out and run time off the clock or when the losing team desperately needs possession for a score.

Faceoffs occur at the beginning of every game and period. A stoppage in play can also result in a faceoff. Officials drop the puck between the sticks of two players after every goal. Faceoffs take place after pucks fly out of play or an injury halts the action. They also happen once the whistle blows for a penalty after the team penalized touches the puck. Not all faceoffs take place at center ice. There are several spots on the playing surface in which the players battle for the puck.

Teammates are not idle during a faceoff. They are positioned beside and behind the two featured players and often are responsible for securing possession. Sometimes they are even called upon to replace a player who has done something illegally in the faceoff circle, such as not positioning themself properly or failing to rest their stick on the ice before the puck is dropped.[45]

Other violations can also result in a player getting kicked off the faceoff circle. Included among them is neglecting to square up one's skates. A player is not allowed to angle their skates to where they want to push the puck once it is dropped by the referee. Another surefire way for an offensive player to get booted out of a faceoff is if they do not allow the defensive player to place their stick on the ice first. A teammate can even force a player to be ejected from a faceoff by entering the circle before the two combatants have had a chance to fight for the puck. Once the puck is dropped, the rest of the players can crash the circle to secure it. Some teams prefer to limit that number, while others drop back to wait for a potential pass.

Penalties are rarely called on faceoffs. A minor bench penalty occurs when a team is called for successive faceoff violations. A player is then sent to the penalty box for two minutes of action, which gives the opposition a power-play opportunity.[46]

There have been debates over the importance of winning faceoffs over the years. They make for intriguing statistical conversations, but some believe they make little difference to the outcome. One might argue that merely securing the puck off faceoffs matters little when teams control the puck so often during games in which they average three or four goals. Players are quite adept at returning possession to their side during back-and-forth action.

One analysis based on research done by Carolina Hurricane assistant coach Eric Tulsky in 2011 furthered the assertion that the results of faceoffs make virtually no impact. It determined that teams breaking even on faceoffs over a full season average about ninety-one points (based on the NHL system of points earned). One study showed that winning fifty more faceoffs than opponents translate into only about one more point. Given that each win results in two points, a team must win one hundred more faceoffs than the opposition to gain the equivalent of one victory from such dominance. That same study further concluded that there is little correlation between winning faceoffs and getting off more shots on goal. Good teams will find a way to secure the puck for shots no matter whether they possess it at the beginning of a play.

The emphasis on analytics and more in-depth statistical analysis has clarified the comparative significance of winning or losing various plays. That includes faceoffs in hockey. Many feel the theory that they only play an important role at the end of tight games when securing the puck is critical makes the most sense.

QUESTION 13: WHAT IS AN "ODD MAN RUSH"?

Bill Keenan grew up a devout Rangers fan in New York City in the 1990s and early 2000s. He yearned to play someday for his favorite team. But the furthest he could advance his career was junior hockey and competing for Harvard before continuing to chase his dream in Sweden.

Along the way he began to write. He gathered humorous and poignant anecdotes about the sport from college teammates and friends through email. Soon, his dream of playing in the NHL was shattered. He returned to the Big Apple and landed a job in finance that he hated.

Keenan remained passionate about hockey. So, he transcribed all the stories about his experience and that of others in the sport and turned it into a book published in 2016 titled *Odd Man Rush: A Harvard Kid's Hockey Odyssey from Central Park to Somewhere in Sweden—with Stops Along the Way*. Four years later, his work was transformed into a feature film.[47]

The book and movie spotlighted a term with which few, aside from ardent hockey fans, are familiar: "odd man rush." It is an offshoot of a "rush," which is a combined attack by more than one player on the team in possession of the puck. It generally includes anywhere from two to five players rushing toward the opposing net in quest of a goal.

An ideal rush is one in which the attacking team gains a competitive advantage by rushing up the ice with more players than the opposition has defenders. That is an odd man rush. The bigger the difference, the more advantageous the odd man rush.

Similar terminology explains other goal-scoring strategies. "Rush the puck" describes when a defenseman handles the prized disc up the ice into the offensive zone to create a scoring opportunity for himself or his teammates. Sometimes the player will skate end to end to increase that possibility. Though the primary task of a defenseman is to protect the net and prevent clear shots on goal more plays have been called in recent years that allow them to play a bigger offensive role. The position was redefined in the late 1960s and early 1970s by such scoring talents as Bobby Orr and has continued to evolve.

Teams try to maximize the offensive threats of defenseman while losing nothing on the other end. Their offensive assignments are mostly limited. They often carry the puck forward only short distances before passing it to a forward and retreating. When defensemen do travel into the offensive zone, the forward must cover for him, because, if the puck is stolen, that scenario can create an odd man rush such as a two-on-one or three-on-one. Any offensive play created off such a disadvantage is known as "off the rush."[48]

A far more critical task of defensemen is to stop rushes into their zone than to initiate them for their teammates. But offensive players are also responsible for preventing attacks on the other end. Among the keys to that chore is backchecking, which refers to chasing puck carriers in transition and impeding their progress without being called for a penalty such as tripping or slashing with the stick. A critical strategy is forcing puck carriers toward the boards rather than letting them skate down the of the rink where they can pass it to skilled shooters on either side.

The term "odd man rush" is basically a colorful description of any player advantage on the offensive end.

QUESTION 14: HOW THICK IS THE ICE IN HOCKEY ARENAS AND HOW IS IT MADE?

Fans who stream into Olympic and NHL arenas to watch their favorite teams rarely consider the effort required to prepare the rinks for competition. And most do not understand or care about the differences between Olympic rinks and NHL rinks. But distinctions do exist.

Olympic hockey is played on a surface measuring two hundred feet long and ninety-eight feet wide. NHL games feature rinks of the same length but only eighty-five feet wide. One major impact is that blue lines in the international sport are six feet farther from the net, thereby increasing the offensive zone. The only exception was the 2010 Games in Vancouver, which was held in NHL arenas. Approval to maintain the dimensions there saved organizers about $10 million in renovation costs.[49]

The league has studied optimal ice thickness, which is more important than casual fans might believe. The surface is three-quarters of an inch thick for a reason. That makes it thick enough to withstand the pressure of teams skating upon it but not thick enough to soften the ice and slow down the game. Thinner, harder ice is preferred because it allows players to move faster and speeds up the action, though outdoor rinks for recreational purposes do not promote speed, which means their ice can be up to one and a half inches thick.

More fascinating is how NHL ice rinks are constructed— sometimes very quickly if arenas are also homes of NBA teams and the rinks must be prepared for battle the following evening. Some might believe that the lone task is pouring a lot of water on the surface and allowing it to freeze. But the process is far more extensive and complex.

Hockey surfaces freeze using an indirect refrigeration system that creates and maintains the optimal temperature. Aided by a network of piles beneath the ice, the device pumps around ten thousand gallons of freezing brine water per minute. Brine water is basically ordinary water mixed with dissolved alkaline salts that provide a bit more thickness. Brine water also freezes at lower temperatures than basic water, allowing it to circulate through the pipes without freezing while still being cold enough to freeze the water atop the concrete floors of the rink.[50]

The procedure of creating the rinks is known as layering the ice. That begins when a thin layer of ice is sprayed over the cold concrete and immediately freezes. Smaller layers of ice are then sprayed atop the first one. Each layer is between one sixteenth and one thirtieth of an inch thick. The process continues until the required thickness of ice is reached. About ten thousand gallons of water are required to finish the job.[51]

At that point, the rink is nearly ready for play. The ice is painted white to contrast with the black puck, then lines and logos are added. The Zamboni finishes the job by scraping the surface and collecting the snow. The machine also places down a sheet of water warmed to about 140 degrees. It does not melt the ice because it freezes quickly, but it further smooths the surface.

The entire process can take up to forty-eight hours. The result is that in some arenas in which basketball and hockey are both played, the ice remains in place at all times and a hardwood court is laid on top of it.

QUESTION 15: HOW DID THE 1980 US OLYMPIC TEAM DEFEAT THE SOVIETS?

What became known as the "Miracle on Ice" after the iconic declaration by then-youthful sports broadcaster Al Michaels—"Do you believe in miracles?"—was among the most shocking upsets in the history of international sports. That a group of college kids could defeat the powerful and heretofore dominant Russian team in the 1980 Olympic semifinal remains memorable more than forty years later for a myriad of reasons.

One centered on an era that proved to be a flash point of the Cold War. Americans needed a dose of patriotism only five years after the end of the divisive Vietnam War and the Watergate scandal, which not only brought down President Richard Nixon but caused cynicism about the US political system. Another landmark event that added to the tension of the turbulent times was the hostage crisis, which weighed heavily in the hearts and minds of Americans as their countrymen were held captive throughout 1980 by Iranian extremists. One issue more directly affecting relations between the United States and Soviet Union was the latter's invasion of Afghanistan, which caused the Americans to boycott the summer Olympic Games held in Russia that year and eventually resulted in the Soviets boycotting the Olympics in Los Angeles four years later.

Politics are ideally put aside in all international competition, particularly the Olympic Games, which is intended to promote brotherhood among all nations. But such had rarely been the case, particularly during the 1972 Summer Games in Munich, when members of the Israeli team were kidnapped by Palestinian terrorists and murdered. The specter of all that was happening politically hung over the Olympic Center in Lake Placid, New York, when the Russians and Americans faced off for a shot at a gold medal game.

That the underdogs boasted any chance to win seemed absurd. The USSR had won all twelve of the previous matchups against the United States since 1960 by a combined score of 127–27. Even in the 1976 Canada Cup, when NHL players competed, the United States scored a mere two goals in losing twice to the Russians. And in the exhibition clash between the two countries at Madison Square Garden in New York a week before the 1980 Olympics began, the Soviets dominated in a 10–3 victory.[52]

That did give the Americans one psychological advantage: their opponents' overconfidence. Russian coach Viktor Tikhonov claimed later that the worst mistake his club made was playing the United States before the Games because its utter dominance caused his players to underestimate their foe. They assumed they were in for an easy victory despite how well the youngest American Olympic team ever (average age of twenty-two) had played in earlier games to reach the semifinals.[53]

Soviet overconfidence turned into panic despite its experience and success advantage when it became apparent early that its supremacy of weeks earlier would not be repeated. Frustration also reared its ugly head when its control of the action did not translate into goals. That factor continued throughout. The Russians finished with fifty-two shot attempts—forty-nine of which were turned away by American goaltender Jim Craig—to just twenty-five for its opponent. They outshot the United States in five-on-five full strength situations, 46–21. Thirty-nine Soviet shots hit their targets, a statistic that screams out the brilliance of Craig under fire. An ESPN study of the game action revealed that they held a 20–7 advantage in unblocked shots from dangerous scoring areas on the ice. Yet the Russians were outscored 3–2 on those shots.

Among the many attractions of the Olympic Games since 1896 has been heroic performances by those unlikely to rise to the occasion. That battle produced several Herculean efforts, as have many in Olympic history, but that of Craig exceeded all. Even the strongest of defenses in hockey have been destroyed by weak goaltending. But Craig kick-saved and glove-saved nearly all that came his way despite being peppered with Soviet shots. He halted six of ten Russian power play shots and what was determined to be eight of ten shots coming from areas of the rink most likely to result in a goal.

Among those who marveled at the goalie was Team USA advance scout Lou Vairo. "Jim Craig played the game of his life," Vairo said. "He was a brilliant goalkeeper and one of the smartest goalies I've ever met." Indeed, Craig's .923 save percentage that fateful day proved far superior to his usual numbers at Boston University and short NHL career.[54]

The USSR team excelled in creating opportunities for an odd man rush, which is somewhat like a fast break in basketball. But the strategies of US coach Herb Brooks limited them. He had confidence in his team's discipline on that end despite its youth. The Americans made certain there were three or four defenders back. That proved critical given the advantage the Soviets had in time controlling the puck. They were constantly harassed and disrupted. The only goal from which a breakaway behind the defense resulted was Alexander Maltsev's breakaway in the second period. The Russians completed fewer than 20 percent of their passes among the eighty-four times they landed the puck in the US zone. They were often forced to settle for longer shots that missed the mark or that Craig saved easily. Brooks had his players well-schooled on the game plan and they executed it better as the clash progressed while gaining confidence in it along the way.

All of which should not detract from their budding talent. The group that stunned the Soviets ended up playing more than six thousand combined games and scoring more than 3,500 goals in the NHL. "I had been away from amateur hockey for 10 years, and . . . I was shocked at the talent level that was available to the Olympic team," said US assistant coach and future New York Rangers general manager Craig Patrick.[55]

Brooks trusted all his players implicitly, giving time on the ice to four lines, all of whom often played during stretches of two minutes. That kept his charges fresh and eager. It also helped the offense take advantage of the few chances it had to score. The US team entered the offensive zone with the puck in less than half of its sixty-nine visits, none of which lasted long. It needed to maximize those opportunities and did. To score four goals given that distinct lack of openings was quite remarkable and a tribute to skill and grit. Mark Johnson fooled typically brilliant Soviet goaltender Vladislav Tretiak by holding the puck a split second longer before sending it past him. The game-winner by Mark Eruzione displayed his skating abilities as he maneuvered in front of the goal and nailed a wrist shot past backup goalie Vladimir Myshkin, who had replaced the failing Tretiak (a move that angered the legend for years), to find the net. "That was a goal scorer's goal," Vairo recalled. "Only a sharpshooter could shoot that."[56]

Thereafter, the United States continued to frustrate the Soviets by dumping the puck into the neutral zone. Craig did the rest. The Russians managed nine shots on goal after the Eruzione goal. None reached their target.

That the Americans completed the Miracle on Ice by defeating Finland for the gold medal is largely forgotten, greatly due to the politics of the time and the Russian hockey dominance of the era. But the players did not care about the political ramifications of their victory.

"We focused on the hockey game," Eruzione said. "We didn't know what was going on around us. We weren't allowed to talk to the media, so we didn't know what was happening other than what was going on in Lake Placid and maybe at home with our family and friends. That was a good thing, because we were shocked by it when we got out into the country and realized: This thing was pretty huge. So, we were in a little village in Lake Placid, and pretty much kept to ourselves, and the task at hand was to play hockey . . . the political climate, that was never discussed . . . To us, it was a hockey game."[57]

That's how it *should* be. But the Cold War and all that made it unfortunately flourish would not allow that game to ever be viewed only as one of the biggest upsets in the history of international sports.

QUESTION 16: HOW DO PLAYERS ON THE BENCH KNOW WHEN TO CHANGE LINES?

First things first. A line consists of three forwards—one center and two wings. They are considered offensive players who compete on the ice with two defensemen and a goaltender.

Among the many unique facets of the sport is that players are allowed to shift in and out of games during the action rather than waiting for stoppages. Their ability to meld and thrive during the flow of the game can sometimes be critical to team success. Clumsy line changes can lead to goals. So sharp awareness by all line mates of assignments such as when and how long to shift and strategic matchups against particular opponents and ensuring that such substitutions will not increase scoring chances defensively are critical.

Unlike premier basketball talent, who typically remain in the court for ten minutes or longer before catching a break and stay active for thirty-five to forty minutes of forty-eight-minute games, hockey players generally shift about every thirty to forty-five seconds. After that amount of time, their performance begins to weaken. The lack of slowdowns or frequent halts in the proceedings, as well as the tremendous energy and stamina with which they must compete, necessitates frequent line changes.[58]

Players understand it. They practice it. They know intuitively when it is time to leave the ice or hop on. Among the exceptions is during a power play, when one might remain active for a minute or a bit longer and offensive players skate less while generally remaining in their ends. But their penalty-killing teammates often switch after thirty seconds because their task is so tiring. It is no wonder that NHL players burn two thousand calories or more every game.[59]

The two most common shifts are those of complete forward lines and two defensemen. Coaches pair talent that work best together, which is why the shifts most often consist of the same forward lines and defenders much of the entire season if they remain consistently effective. But other factors are involved. Offensive lines can serve different purposes. Teams use four separate groups. One or two might be best at scoring. Another could be most adept at stopping the best offensive talent on an opponent. A fourth line can be best at establishing a hard forecheck, which in turn establishes momentum for more offensive-minded teammates. Defensemen generally stay on the ice before shifting a bit longer—but not much.

Indeed, shifting on and off the rink is quite strategic and based on opponent strengths and weaknesses. A forward group and defensive duo unlikely to score might be used simply to stymie the premier offensive unit on the other side. Or because the best offensive line on one team is simply inferior to that of the opponent. Two defenders often arrive on the ice to combat the other team's top offensive talent. Such matchups are continuous during the course of a game.

There is one problem, and that is timing. Changes must be executed only when it's safe. A player can't skate to the bench when the other team is threatening to score. Changeovers take place only when the puck is as far away from that team's goal as possible. Players do their best to ensure it by skating just over the red line (to avoid icing) and shooting the puck with no legitimate intent to put into the net before heading in, thereby buying time for their offensive or defensive teammates to enter. Generally, at least one player remains on the ice until it is safe to leave.

That arrangement is not always possible. Teams do not always substitute entire lines. A shift might only safely allow one or two players to change at the same time, such as when a line gets trapped in their own zone and the puck comes out past the blue line, thereby giving enough time to change over one or two players, but not the entire line and never the defensemen, who are busy working to prevent a goal.[60]

Hockey players at the NHL and top international levels are simply too skilled to risk awkward for mistimed line changes. Teams practice substitutions but poor execution that leads to goals against occasionally occur. Boston Bruins forward Brad Marchand notoriously made a bad line change in Game 7 of the 2019 NHL Stanley Cup Finals. It cost his team a goal in their loss to the St. Louis Blues.[61]

Given the complexities of line changes, it is no wonder that rules differ in lower levels of hockey. In most recreational and beginner hockey leagues such maneuvers are timed. A buzzer might go off to signal a shift. Coaches are more animated and active in their approach, sometimes calling players on and off the ice to ensure proper execution. They often use line changes not so much for a competitive advantage but to give many or even all his charges equal playing time. In the NHL, the practice is based on matchups and placing the top talent into action.[62]

The length of shifts also differs. Professional players generally stay on the ice for only about forty-five seconds and even less as tired legs take over in the third period or otherwise late in games. Recreational players often go full tilt for up to two minutes before being replaced. The most opportune and sometimes fortunate moment for a line change at all levels is after a whistle halts the action.

Speed and even location in embarking on a shift can be critical. It should be done as quickly as possible. That is why NHL players hoist themselves over the bench to get on the ice rather than using the gate. Forwards position themselves closest to the opponent's net for fastest entry into the preferred zone while defensemen enter through the gate closest to their team's goaltender.

The process is fun to watch, particularly for those unfamiliar with the idiosyncrasies of the sport and for those witnessing it for the first time. It adds to the excitement and nonstop action of the game.

QUESTION 17: WHAT POEM PASSAGE IS ON THE WALL IN MONTREAL'S LOCKER ROOM?

Much can be debated about the NHL. But there is little argument regarding its most iconic and successful franchise historically. It is the Montreal Canadiens.

Though that club had gone thirty seasons without a Stanley Cup championship heading into 2022 and only reached the finals once during that stretch (in 2021) its dominance reached nearly mythical proportions in earlier times. The Canadiens were a dynasty. They won twenty-four crowns, including fifteen from 1956 to 1979. Only twice in those twenty-four seasons were they extended to seven games in the title round. They lost just one Cup final during that period—a defeat to archrival Toronto. Only the baseball Yankees and basketball Celtics can lay claim to similarly dominant dynasties in North American major sports history.

The result has been a feeling of pride and tradition unmatched in professional hockey. The move from the legendary Montreal Forum to the Molson Centre (now called the Bell Centre) in 1996 evaporated some of those feelings, and certainly the team itself lost some of its luster under the weight of expansion and greater parity. But the franchise has remained iconic for its history and onetime dominance. And that is felt by visitors to home games despite the change in venues.

The organization made sure of that when it carefully re-created the Canadiens locker room at the new arena. It even launched a virtual visit site for fans in 2006. Included were portraits of the forty-one Canadien players to have been honored with Hockey Hall of Fame inductions. That gave ordinary fans access to plaques honoring such stars as Maurice "the Rocket" Richard, Jean Beliveau, and Guy Lafleur, all of which were lined high up on the dressing room walls.

But most intriguing is a verse taken from a John McCrae poem titled "In Flanders Field." It reads: "To you from failing hands we throw the torch, be yours to hold it high." That quote has remained in the Canadiens locker room since the 1952–1953 season. It was put there by then–general manager Frank Selke Sr., who foresaw possible motivation for his team coached by Dick Irvin, which won the Stanley Cup that year. The words were placed high on the wall in the locker room and have inspired the players ever since.[63]

The hundredth anniversary of the poem was celebrated throughout Canada in 2015. Anong those authoring essays in a book titled *In Flanders Field: Writing on War, Loss and Remembrance* was legendary Canadiens goaltender Ken Dryden.

McCrae was a soldier, field surgeon, and poet. He was motivated to write the poem after a close friend perished in battle in Ypres. Soon thereafter it gained fame throughout North America and Europe. It encapsulated feelings of valor, grief and remembrance for the fallen. It read:

In Flanders fields the poppies blow
Between the crosses, row on row,
That mark our place; and in the sky
The larks, still bravely singing, fly
Scarce heard amid the guns below.

We are the Dead. Short days ago
We lived, felt dawn, saw sunset glow,
Loved and were loved, and now we lie,
In Flanders fields.

Take up our quarrel with the foe:
To you from failing hands we throw
The torch; be yours to hold it high.
If ye break faith with us who die
We shall not sleep, though poppies grow
In Flanders fields.[64]

Dryden, who starred for the Canadiens throughout the 1970s, wrote in the book about how the poem arrived on the wall of the locker room. It sits rather majestically around the circular wall near the ceiling and adds to the legend of the franchise itself. It is not alone in its feeling of pride and history. The Montreal clubhouse also boasts plaques of all its Hall of Famers, which proves inspirational, especially to those who enter for the first time. Among them was center Nate Thompson, who had played thirteen years in the NHL before a trade sent him from the Kings to the Canadiens in 2019. He was overwhelmed by such feelings upon his arrival.

"I kind of felt like a young guy again, coming into a franchise like this, seeing the room, seeing all the history," Thompson said after his first practice with the team. "I kind of just walked around the locker room for a few minutes, tried to take it all in and enjoy it. I looked around a little bit this morning and saw the 200 Hall of Famers you guys have here. I didn't know what jersey number I would be wearing because every jersey's retired here. But it's awesome."[65]

The Canadiens lost their luster in the late 1990s and beyond, falling short of the playoffs ten times in twenty-three seasons through 2022 and securing no titles since 1993. But their status as the greatest team in NHL history remains unquestioned, and the aura of legend that surrounds the franchise will never die. The poem and plaques on the wall of their locker room will likely ensure that for decades to come.

QUESTION 18: HOW ARE NHL RINKS LAID OUT?

First, a little etymology. The word "rink" is based on the Scottish word meaning "course." The first hockey rinks were constructed for the sport of curling.

Rinks are rectangular. But importantly to the sports, they feature rounded edges that keep the puck moving and create a sense of nonstop action. The edges of the rink are marked by walls up to four feet high called boards. Acrylic glass extends above the boards to safeguard the fans while also allowing them to see the game clearly. The barriers extend vertically eight feet on the ends of the rink and five feet on the sides. The higher protection near the goals, as well as nets that rise another eighteen feet above the glass, prevent pucks off deflected or errant shots from hitting and harming spectators.[66]

The rinks of the NHL, which differ in size from those used in Olympic and other international hockey, are painted with three types of lines, all of which cover the entire width of the ice. The red center line divides the surface into two one-hundred-foot halves. Two thick blue lines extend across the rink twenty-five feet from the center lines. That creates a fifty-foot neutral zone in the middle of the rink. There is also another red line on both ends of the ice painted parallel to the front of both goals. It shows the line the puck must cross for a goal to be scored.

One zone aside from offensive, defensive, and neutral has been added in more recent years. And that is a trapezoid behind the nets in which the goaltenders are allowed to handle the puck. It was introduced in the NHL in 2005 to reduce the area in which the most goalies can take advantage of their passing and puck-handling skills.

Two other areas easily visible to spectators in hockey arenas and that are, of course, not in play are the benches and penalty boxes. The benches extend the width of the neutral zone and end at either side of the center line. The players on the bench are not shielded by glass as they must be free to hop over into action or use the door to enter and exit play.

One bench just off the ice houses scorekeepers and two others await players who have committed penalties. All three of those benches are protected by glass. Players in penalty boxes resume action through a door.

Because of the small size of the puck and continuous action of the game, hockey can be a difficult sport to follow in the arena. Fans fortunate enough to sit closest to the glass pay top dollar to get the ultimate experience. They can even feel the physical nature of the game, particularly when players are checked into the boards that are merely a few feet away.

QUESTION 19: WHAT IS THE "MARTIN BRODEUR TRAPEZOID RULE"?

Martin Brodeur could be excused if he believed the NHL was picking on him. The New Jersey Devils goaltender and future Hall of Famer had become so adept as a puck-handler in initiating offense that the league created a new rule to curb his impact. The introduction of a trapezoid area that limited goaltender access to the puck would forever be known as the "Brodeur Rule."

His brilliant twenty-four-year career was marked with team and personal triumphs. He broke NHL records with 691 wins and 125 shutouts. He led the Devils to three championships. He captured Rookie of the Year honors in 1994 and continued to earn post-season hardware. Like all goaltenders, his primary greatness was based on his ability to stop pucks from flying into the net.

The new rule, which went into effect in 2005 after the lockout killed the previous season, prevented players from dumping the puck off to their goalies, who in turn began serving as a third defenseman. It disallowed all puck-handling and passing by goalies outside a small zone behind the net. The new edict read as follows:

> A goaltender may not play the puck outside a designated area behind the net. This area is defined by lines that begin on the goal line, six feet from each goal post, and extend diagonally to points 28 feet apart at the end boards. Should a goalie play the puck outside this area behind the goal line, a minor penalty for delay of game will be imposed. The determining factor will be the position of the puck.[67]

The rule was intended to encourage more offense, but Brodeur felt it targeted him and a few others elite puck-handling goaltenders while numbing their talents. "If they had 30 Martin Brodeurs out there, that rule wouldn't be there; nobody would have voted for it," he said. "There are just too many teams that didn't have these goalies that were ready to make sure the guys that were affecting the game weren't able to do it anymore."[68]

Brodeur added that the new rule would reward bad dumps rather than prevent the practice. He cited more dumping off to goaltenders if they cannot play the puck. But longtime NHL General Manager Brian Burke held a different opinion. "The game was turning into a tennis match," he complained. "You'd dump it in and the goalie would throw it out and now with the soft chip into the corner it turns into a puck battle and a forecheck opportunity, which is what we wanted."[69]

It certainly wasn't what Brodeur wanted. "You can't be happy, taking away something I've worked on all my life to do and help my teammates and help my defense," he said. "It's just part of me, playing the puck . . . The NHL wants to show the talent to their fans and stuff. And I think this is not doing it. I think it goes the other way around. It goes taking away a talent from guys. There's a lot of guys that can't play the puck, and that doesn't affect them."[70]

If the NHL was indeed seeking to create more offense, the rule served an immediate purpose. Average goals per team per game jumped from 2.57 to 3.08 the year it was instituted but did not reach that level again until the 2021−2022 season.

QUESTION 20: WHAT ARE THE PRIMARY NHL POSTSEASON AWARDS?

Ask most sports fans who do not follow the NHL closely and they can at least identify the name of its ultimate trophy. They know that the revered Stanley Cup is annually presented to the league champion. But they could not cite the names of any other postseason awards or what they signify. And there are many.

Several are team honors. Among them is the Presidents' Trophy, which is earned by the team with the top point total during the regular season. The long playoff slog has generally stopped that winner from claiming the league championship. The only exceptions from 2003 to 2022 were the 2008 Detroit Red Wings and 2013 Chicago Blackhawks.

Trophies are also awarded to teams that emerge from the Eastern Conference to play for the Stanley Cup. It receives a trophy named after the Prince of Wales, who donated it in 1924. It became known as the Prince of Wales Trophy in 1993. The Western Conference winner is presented the Clarence S. Campbell Bowl, which was named after the NHL president from 1946 to 1977.

All the individual awards serve as a road map to NHL history. The selections, picked since 1967 by the Professional Hockey Writers Association, are a who's who of the all-time greats, particularly those earning them in multiple years.

The most prestigious is the Hart Memorial Trophy, which was donated to the league in 1924 by Dr. David Hart and named after his son Cecil Hart, who served as coach and general manager of the Canadiens. Originally called the Hart Trophy, it was set to retire in 1960 but instead was renamed to strengthen the honor of its originator. Immortal scoring machine Wayne Gretzky holds the record by winning it nine times (including an outrageous eight in a row from 1980 to 1987), but only three recipients were not ticketed for the Hockey Hall of Fame upon retirement. Among them was Tommy "Cowboy" Anderson, who earned it in 1942 by scoring forty-one points as a defenseman and despite his Brooklyn Americans finishing last.[71]

Awarded since 1965, the Conn Smythe Trophy was named after the former Toronto Maple Leafs coach, president, and owner-governor. It honors who the hockey writers deem to be the Most Valuable Player of the postseason. Only five players not on the winning team in the Stanley Cup final have earned it and none from 2003 through 2022. It has, however, provided far more balance—Gretzky only captured it twice. The lone three-time winner was goaltender Patrick Roy, who never snagged it for the same team. He won it with Edmonton in 1986, Montreal in 1993, and Colorado in 2001, all of which accentuated the length and brilliance of his career.

The history of the Conn Smythe Trophy is indicative of team dominance during particular eras. Four different New York Islanders (Bryan Trottier, Butch Goring, Mike Bossy, and Billy Smith) captured it as the team embarked on a four-year dynasty from 1980 to 1983.

Since 1933, the Calder Memorial Trophy has been given to the top rookie. It is named after 1930s and early 1940s NHL President Frank Calder. Players who competed in twenty-five or fewer games prior to the season are eligible to win. The Maple Leafs led the way through 2022 with ten winners but only one (future Hart Memorial Trophy winner Auston Matthews in 2017) since 1966.

The Vezina Trophy was dedicated to fallen Canadiens goalie Georges Vezina, who collapsed during a game in 1925 and died of tuberculosis two months later. It is voted upon by league general managers and presented to the premier goaltender after every season. In the 1960s and 1970s, the honor was most often bestowed upon multiple players from the same team. But that practice stopped thereafter. Various goalies won it during periods of domination, including Dominik Hasek of the Buffalo Sabres and Martin Brodeur of the New Jersey Devils. Only Sergie Bobrovsky of the Columbus Blue Jackets earned it twice from 2011 to 2022.

Another position award is the James Norris Memorial Trophy, which is named after the owner-president of the Detroit Red Wings from 1932 to 1953 and was launched the following year. It is given annually to the top all-around defenseman and, not surprisingly, was dominated by Boston Bruins superstar Bobby Orr in the late 1960s into the mid-1970s. Orr, who redefined the position with his explosiveness on the offensive end, won it every year from 1968 to 1975. Others have also controlled the honor. Montreal star Doug Harvey won it every year but one from 1955 to 1962. Nicklas Lidstrom, who helped transform the Red Wings into a powerhouse, earned it six times from 2001 to 2008.

The Jack Adams Award is voted upon by the NHL Broadcasters Association and has basically served as Coach of the Year since 1974. The organization has been generous to many—only Red Wings coach Jacque Demers (1987 and 1988) won it in consecutive years through 2022.

The NHL does not stop there. It distributes many lesser annual postseason awards named after legends. They are selected by various panels and honor a wide range of achievement both on and off the ice.

Among them are the Maurice Richard Trophy (top goal scorer), King Clancy Trophy (best humanitarian), Ted Lindsay Award (most outstanding player as voted upon by the Players Association), Mark Messier NHL Leadership Trophy, Jim Gregory GM of the Year, and Bill Masterson Memorial Trophy (exemplifying the ideals of perseverance, sportsmanship, and dedication to the sport).

The NHL values tradition, and that is demonstrated by the legendary names recognized by its postseason awards. But new legends arrive on the hockey scene every decade. Perhaps—such as in the case of Messier, who starred with the Oilers, Rangers, and Canucks from 1979 to 2004—they too will be so honored in future generations.

QUESTION 21: WHAT IS THE TWO-PASS RULE AND WHY DID THE NHL DUMP IT?

2005 was a big year for changes in the NHL. The league was coming off a lost season after a lockout and yearned to bring back angry fans. So modifications were made to add offense into the sport, including the Martin Brodeur Trapezoid Rule.

Another was the elimination of the two-line pass rule, which is when play is halted because a player in the defensive zone sends the puck past both the blue line and red line to a teammate unless the receiver has not yet reached the red line and must catch up to it.

The two-line pass rule had been in effect since 1943. It was implemented to stop teams from cherry-picking and having a player hang or roam around the offensive end to receive passes for uncontested shots on goal. But that proved more of an advantage for defenses, which eventually learned to send all five players into the offensive neutral zone to prevent opponents from advancing the puck up the ice via passing or skating. That became known as the "neutral zone trap." Teams understood that if a pass did somehow elude them, it would fall victim to the two-line pass rule. It was a win-win situation for defense. The result was low-scoring games that hockey fans considered boring and did not add ardent followers to the ranks.

The two-line pass rule made more sense in the 1940s when goalie pads were small, making it harder to stop shots. All padding from the legs to the helmets were significantly smaller compared to the modern equipment. The two-line pass rule helped offset that offensive advantage.

The 1994 lockout brought a sense of urgency. So did goal-scoring averages of just over five per game. Attendance had dropped. So had TV ratings. Networks ignored hockey. The result was plummeting revenue and disgruntled fans, coaches, general managers, and players. The NHL board needed to generate excitement, which often means adding offense in all sports. The result was elimination of the two-line pass rule. Players were given the green light to send long passes down the ice, giving the game a more open feel and faster pace.

Hockey has never been the same since. But that does not mean the two-line pass rule has had its desired effect. After an initial bump in scoring—it increased about one goal per game during the 2005–2006 season—the numbers began to fall consistently for a decade and have only risen again since 2016 to levels still significantly down from what the league experienced in the 1980s, when scoring was at its peak. Strategy battles between offense and defense have been fought forever in all sports and certainly played a role in NHL defenses becoming more adept at combating the elimination of the two-line pass rule.

That does not mean it has not piqued some interest in the sport. The motivation for ending the rule was not merely to increase goal scoring. It was to limit stoppages in the action and create a more free-flowing game. Players have been better able to use their speed due to more open territory on the ice. They can stand behind their goal, drill a pass to an open teammate positioned in front of the opposition blue line, and head in for a breakaway. Also more common are defensemen in their zone hitting wingers in stride entering the game on a line change. Passes that connect to the sticks of teammates returning to action have sometimes easily skated past defenders for shots on goal.

One result has been the rise of fast skaters. The prime example as the 2010s waned and into the 2020s was Edmonton Oiler center Connor McDavid, who averaged 108 points (goals and assists) over his first six full seasons and earned the Hart Memorial Trophy in both 2017 and 2021. McDavid took advantage of the more open game to use his speed and stick-handling talents to work his way in for open shots and the net and set up his teammates to score.

One drawback for players, though one that creates a bit more drama for fans, is that the elimination of the two-line pass rule has created a greater sense of danger. The more wide-open action resulted in more and harder open-ice hits and injuries. Longer passes give defenders more time to zero in on their targets. Another negative in the hearts and minds of hockey purists is the belief that it has reduced the need for skill. Their contention is that as speedier skaters simply whiz past defenders, the requirement for sharp passing and puck-handling is lessened.

The move by the NHL inspired other leagues to follow suit. The American Hockey League (AHL), which boasts minor-league affiliates for the parent clubs, also killed off the two-line pass rule, as did the Kontinental Hockey League and various junior leagues such as the Ontario Hockey League and United States Hockey League.

The International Ice Hockey Federation, the governing body for ice hockey that hosts many tournaments, including the World Championships and World Junior Championships, also ended the two-line pass rule but considered reinstating it in 2014. The proposal to do so was rejected.

Most new rules in all sports encounter both negative and positive results. The removal of the two-line pass rule has not enhanced scoring and has made the game a bit more dangerous for the players, but it has quickened its pace and increased action.[72]

QUESTION 22: WHY DID SCORING RISE AND FALL IN THE 1980S AND BEYOND?

Like disco music from the decade before, it came and went. It was a historical hiccup, an anomaly. It was the 1980s in the NHL, years of unprecedented scoring.

It was an offensive decade, but to hockey purists it was "offensive" in a negative sense. The average total goals per game reached eight during the 1981–1982 season. That was the year when the incomparable Wayne Gretzky sent ninety-two shots—more than one per game—into the net. He tallied an incredible 215 points in 1985–1986. Meanwhile, Islanders star Mike Bossy was in the midst of a nine-year run of scoring at least fifty-one goals.

Explosive offensive talents, however, does not offer a full explanation. Some with mediocre abilities powered pucks past goaltenders at alarming rates. It was no wonder that no goalie earned Vezina awards more than once throughout the 1980s. There were simply not many good ones. That honor became a popularity contest rather than deserved acclaim. Established Edmonton standout Grant Fuhr snagged it in 1988 despite saving just 88 percent of all shots on goal.

Such goal-scoring outputs seemed mind-boggling around the turn of the twenty-first century and well beyond. Point leaders in more recent years pale in comparison to the explosions of Gretzky, Bossy, and Penguins superstar Mario Lemieux to follow. The highest total from 1996 through 2022 was tallied by Tampa Bay Lightning right wing Nikita Kucherov, who not only earns the award for having a name most like a former Soviet leader but scored a league-high 128 points during the 2018–2019 season.

So, what happened? Though scoring rates had been fluctuating for decades, the dramatic increase in the 1980s and drop thereafter was certainly odd. Many factors contributed to this historical anomaly.

Among them was smaller goaltender equipment in the 1980s. It evolved in the 1990s. Shoulder pads became far larger. Leg pads grew from small-pillow size to huge, extending well beyond the top of the knee. Trappers (otherwise known as catch gloves and worn on the nondominant hand to help stop incoming pucks) also got bigger, as did jerseys and hockey pants. It all added up to smaller open targets for shots on goal. That was not the biggest reason for decreased scoring by the 1990s but certainly a contribution.

They also grew. Shorter and smaller netminders such as 5'7" Allan Bester or 5'5" Darren Pang disappeared and were replaced by bigger ones. Most modern goaltenders are at least six feet tall. Though hockey players at all positions are a bit taller and wider in recent years, the change has been more pronounced among goalies.

There is a reason for that metamorphosis. Goaltenders in the 1970 and 1980s required more agility. They had to track the puck and then quickly extend a limb in front of it for a kick or glove save. Smaller goalies tended to be nimbler. But times have changed. A new style emerged in the 1990s that proved more effective. Netminders in that decade and beyond played angles. They dropped down to cover the bottom half of the net and let the puck hit them.

That strategy left open only a few inches of empty net over the shoulders, especially since goaltenders themselves were much bigger. Few shooters were accurate enough to nail such a smaller area. Rather than keep the puck alive for putbacks with kick saves, the new tactic allowed goaltenders to stop them in their tracks, where they simply died. So, though goaltenders still need quick reflexes, they have forced offensive players to take a different tack.

Where in the 1980s shooters most often wound up for big blasts, in more modern times their approach is to maneuver the puck to move goalies from side to side and open a bit more space or fire one in and hope for a rebound.

However, not all reasoning for lower scores after the 1980s center on goaltenders and the neutral-zone trap, which was merely one aspect of massive changes in goal-stopping strategies. Defenses and defensemen assignments became more complex. Before the 1990s, a winger might be told simply to cover the sideboards and watch your man. Thereafter, players needed to understand precisely where on the ice they had to be and when. The expanded use of film study resulted in more detailed analysis of offensive tendencies and proved the best ways and means of stopping them. They were aided by assistant coaches who broke down videos and detailed the most effective tactics.

That has led to game plans and player procurement with a greater focus on defense. The best defensive teams win, especially in the playoffs. One example is the Devils, who drove opponents crazy in the early 2000s with their sophisticated neutral zone trap and snagged the Stanley Cup twice during that era. The 2010 Chicago Blackhawks, who captured the crown despite allowing 2.82 goals per game throughout the postseason, is a rarity. No Stanley Cup champion surrendered more than that over the next decade—the 2012 Kings gave up a mere 1.5 goals per game in 2012. Offered hockey writer Brendan Azoff:

> Defense has to be the priority for any team looking to make an elongated appearance in the Stanley Cup Playoffs. The grueling nature of the games come postseason time make defensive systems paramount for a team's success. The organizations that can best eliminate their oppositions top-flight forwards ultimately have the most success.[73]

The revolution in goalie equipment and size not only shrunk open spaces of the net but also diminished the portion of the ice from which players can legitimately shoot and score. That allows defenders to cover less ground. They can collapse into even smaller areas in front of the goal. That too resulted in more shots being blocked before they even reach the netminder and fewer goals overall.

Yet another factor is conditioning. Teams rarely score by catching defenders off guard anymore. Defensemen in the 1980s and earlier often conserved energy on the ice after longer shifts and only went all out when scoring opportunities arose. Now shorter shifts and great endurance due to better conditioning prevent goals due to defensemen taken by surprise or simply getting beat.

Even economics have snuck into the picture. Premier offensive talent costs big bucks, and it's all about winning anyway. So, teams can save money by piecing together a roster featuring effective defenders headed by a defensive-oriented coach. The strategy can be effective given that sixteen of the thirty-two teams quality for the playoffs. Once that begins, anything can happen—and the best defensive clubs thrive in the postseason anyway.

Officiating also played a role. They often began looking the other way in the 1990s on obstruction, which became a common tactic known as "clutch and grab." Defenders positioned themselves to obstruct a particular puck carrier at a certain spot and time. The harassment resulted in either stealing the puck or knocking it away. Sometimes officials even ignored what basically amounted to tackles on the ice. The NHL addressed the problem after the lockout in 2005—along with a myriad of other issues—in seeking to increase scoring. They reminded referees about the obligations regarding obstructions.[74]

The 1980s was the perfect storm for scoring. Expansion and the adding of teams from the defunct World Hockey Association seemed to weaken defenses. The NHL boasted some of its most explosive offensive players and lacked strong goaltending. The only Hall of Fame goalies who stepped foot on the ice during that decade were Edmonton Oilers star Grant Fuhr and New York Islanders mainstay Billy Smith. Top European players who would strengthen defenses had barely begun making their way onto league rosters.

It did not last long. Scoring had already dissipated by the late 1980s. But for those who craved watching pucks being blasted into the net, it sure was a fun era.

QUESTION 23: WHAT HAPPENED TO THE WORLD HOCKEY ASSOCIATION?

The 1967 NHL expansion left uninvited cities thirsting for hockey. It hesitated to add more teams—it had received enough criticism for doubling from six to twelve. It had taken four decades to expand at all. But television ratings and attendance were rising.

All of which created the notion that a rival to the NHL could thrive. Enter the World Hockey Association in 1971. It was no fly-by-night league. WHA leaders had every intention of competing with the established circuit. And that meant spending big bucks to steal premier talent. Such superstars as Chicago Black Hawks winger Bobby Hull (Winnipeg Jets), Philadelphia Flyers goaltender Bernie Parent (Philadelphia Blazers), and Boston Bruins goalie Gerry Cheevers (Cleveland Crusaders) signed with WHA clubs immediately with more to follow. The $2.75 million contract inked by Hull was the biggest in professional hockey history at the time.

The WHA shot for the moon. It did not merely place franchises in smaller cities to avoid competing with the NHL. It opened for business in direct competition with such clubs as the Blazers, first-year champion New England Whalers, New York Raiders, Los Angeles Sharks, and Chicago Cougars. But it also gave major league hockey to cities yearning for one like Cleveland, Ottawa, Quebec, Winnipeg, Houston, Minneapolis, and Alberta. Notable is that the WHA linked heavily with Canada but did not try to compete with legendary NHL franchises in Montreal and Toronto.

Any hopes that the WHA could compete for the entertainment dollar against their hockey-playing brethren were quickly dashed. The New England Whalers led the new league in attendance the first year at 6,981 in attendance per game. That was lower than all but the lowly California Golden Seals of the NHL. Every other NHL club averaged at least ten thousand spectators per game. The WHA All-Star Game in Quebec City attracted just 5,435 fans despite the inclusion of superstars Hull and former Montreal Canadiens star J. C. Tremblay while the annual NHL classic packed Madison Square Garden.

Undeterred by mediocre attendance, the WHA declared its first year a rousing success and continued to tinker. It placed a franchise in Toronto and moved the Blazers to Vancouver to strengthen its Canadian impact. The latter led the league in attendance in its first year but the former simply could not compete with the NHL Maple Leafs and failed to draw more than five thousand per game despite a winning record.

Perhaps the biggest splash by the WHA aside from the initial signing of Hull was the addition of legend Gordie Howe to the Houston Aeros in 1973. That team stayed on a roll by drafting his sons Mark and Marty. But none of them constituted a blow to the NHL, as the older Howe had been retired for two years. And the Aeros only managed to draw 6,811 fans per game in his first season. The team failed to compete financially, motivating the Howes to move to New England and join the Whalers.

The WHA continued to expand—perhaps too quickly—in its desire to compete. But many teams left for other venues or folded due to economic hardship. Included in 1975 were those that had been in existence for a short time such as the Chicago Cougars, Los Angeles Sharks, Michigan Stags, and Baltimore Blades. The Denver Spurs, Minnesota Fighting Saints, and Ottawa Civics soon fell by the wayside. The Cleveland Crusaders and San Diego Mariners followed suit in 1977.

By that time, the league was in financial trouble. Many of the players who had jumped ship from the NHL returned. Never mind that in one final act of desperation in 1978 the Edmonton Oilers of the WHA become home to offensively explosive young superstars Mark Messier and the Great One—Wayne Gretzky. The fans of that team responded by leading the league in attendance at 11,255 per game, but none of the competition averaged more than nine thousand. The WHA became a proving ground for young talent rather than a legitimate rival to the NHL. It was on its last legs.

The merciful ending arrived when the league folded in June 1979 with six franchises remaining—the Cincinnati Stingers, Birmingham Bulls, Edmonton Oilers, New England Whalers, Quebec Nordiques, and Winnipeg Jets. That only three played in the United States proved the league's failure to maintain viability in that country. The NHL absorbed Edmonton, Hartford, Quebec, and Winnipeg and paid $1.5 million in compensation to the other two.

But though the upstart league hung around for only eight seasons, it certainly made an impact. Its teams lured European talent, inspiring the NHL to do the same. The WHA earned some credit for turning the NHL into an international hotbed. The rival also provided competition for players and forced the NHL to raise its salary structure.

The WHA did not succeed in the long run. But given the miserable failures of renegade leagues in other sports—notably the USFL and XFL in football—and its ability to lure top players away from the NHL, it was not a disaster. It could be considered as a rival in the same category with the American Basketball Association, which lasted roughly the same number of years and wound up with four franchises in the NBA after it folded.

QUESTION 24: FROM WHERE ARE MOST NHL PLAYERS DRAFTED?

The date was June 5, 1963. That is when the NHL held its first player draft.

Other major sports leagues had been picking players rather than scouting, scrambling, and competing to sign them for many years. The NFL draft was launched in 1936. The NBA had been making its selections since 1950. The NHL beat only the MLB, which hosted its first draft in 1967.

Most hockey players selected hone their skills at the junior hockey or collegiate levels. Others are drafted out of Europe. Those choices can be a bit riskier if a particular talent decides to remain overseas.

The first European players selected included Swedish defenseman Borge Salming, who was taken in the sixth round of the 1973 draft by the Toronto Maple Leafs and emerged as a nine-time all-star before his induction into the Hockey Hall of Fame. His greatness inspired an influx of European talent into the upstart World Hockey Association and eventually the NHL. It was previously believed in North America that European players outside Russia (no Soviet bloc players could have been drafted during the Cold War) lacked the talent and toughness to compete in that league.[75]

Perhaps the most coveted Soviet player forced to ignore overtures from the NHL was super goaltender Vladislav Tretiak. His brilliance shone at the international level. He was drafted by the Montreal Canadiens in 1983, but the Soviet government refused to allow him to leave.

More European players have been targeted on draft day as time has marched on. One example was in 2022, when two players from that continent were taken first. Montreal selected explosive Finnish scorer Juraj Slafkovsky first overall, and the New Jersey Devils followed by plucking defenseman Simon Nemec out of Slovakia. Those with experience in pro leagues overseas are considered the most NHL-ready and therefore least risky, though the adjustment to the NHL rules and style of play, as well as living in the United States or Canada full-time, can prove difficult.

The percentage of players drafted by NHL teams out of college has increased in recent years. Collegiate hockey powers such as Michigan, Minnesota, Boston College Boston University, North Dakota, and Wisconsin produce the most pro-ready talent. Franchise general managers have most often preferred to pick those who have proven themselves at the top junior hockey levels. But times have changed. Wolverines standout Owen Power became the first college player to be picked first overall in fifteen years in 2021 when he was snagged by the Buffalo Sabres. There were none from 1963 to 1985.[76]

Despite the increase in drafted European and college players, junior leagues remain factories of highly scouted talent. Canadian and northern American teams such as the London Knights, Kelowna Rockets, Kitchener Rangers, Portland Winterhawks, and Flint Firebirds have stocked NHL rosters with some of its finest players for decades.

The percentage of college players peppering those rosters continued to grow into the third decade of the century. By the end of the 2021–2022 season, a record 349 had competed, shattering the mark of 327 from three years earlier. Fifteen were deemed talented enough to have made their debut after playing college hockey in 2021. The total number of college players represented about 38 percent of those who made at least one appearance in an NHL game.

Some of them were Europeans, who continued to increase their presence. Canada has remained the most prolific producer of NHL talent, but the number has been shrinking. A total of 294 Canadian players were on rosters at the start of the 2022–2023 season. The numbers of Europeans (213) barely exceeded those from the United States (202). Sweden was the biggest contributor with 67, followed by Russia (40), Finland (33), Czech Republic (30), and Switzerland (9).

Though the number of college players in the NHL has increased with time, those that last honed their talents in junior leagues in Canada and the United States (junior leagues also exist in Europe) continued to make them a major proving ground and hotbed for scouts. Top teenagers in junior programs often make college hockey their next step to raise their stock for the NHL draft. The higher level of competition among those in the premier college programs is better suited to improve skills. Players are skating against older, bigger, stronger, and faster competition than found at most junior levels. That is also why an increasing number of Europeans travel overseas to compete at the college level, mostly in the United States.

QUESTION 25: HOW DID GREAT BRITAIN WIN OLYMPIC GOLD IN 1936?

First things first. We're talking men's hockey here. Canada and the United States have so dominated the women's game that their teams have captured every gold medal through 2022 since hockey became an Olympic sport in 1998.

Canada, Russia, and the United States (mostly the first two) ruled internationally through 1992. They won every Olympic championship but one until 1994 after the Winter Games began in 1920. But the fall of the Soviet Union—though what became known as the "Olympic Athletes from Russia" team snagged gold in 1992 and 2018—contributed to other European countries winning it all.

The lone break in the dominance of the Big Three occurred at the 1936 Olympics (allowed, disgracefully, to be held in Germany during the Nazi era—as were the Summer Games). That is when Great Britain stunned Canada in the final.

It would not have taken place in Germany had dictator Adolf Hitler held to his original objections. Before becoming chancellor in 1933, he objected to the notion of his nation hosting the event, condemning it as "a play inspired by Judaism which cannot possibly be put on in a Reich ruled by National Socialists." But minister of propaganda Joseph Goebbels envisioned the Olympics as a means of gaining acceptance and legitimacy around the world. After taking control of the nation, Hitler consented. Anti-Jewish signs were quietly hauled away, and the Nazis put their most tolerant foot forward to welcome the international community.[77]

Included was the British hockey team, which had previously fared no better than third in 1924 and had yet to even play in a gold medal game. That Canada was destined to earn another crown seemed to be a given–that country had already won it four times.

A wave of hockey interest and talent spurred by the bronze medal performance in 1924 and fourth-place effort four years later did raise British hopes. Whereas previously only the Manchester Ice Palace staged training and matches, now several other cities, including London, joined in. Attendance at games featuring the best Britain had to offer often reached ten thousand. Hockey players gained motivation through payouts greater than what soccer players in that country earned. Seasoned foreigners, including those from Canada, were recruited as players and coaches. Among them was Canadian Percy Nicklin, who was eventually appointed manager of the British national team.

Further inspiration was provided by that team from a third-place finish at the 1935 World Championships. The influx of foreign talent raised their level of play. The Brits fell to Canada by an encouraging score of 4–2 in the first stage, but reality set in with a 6–0 defeat to the same dominant club in the final group. That did not stop Canadian hockey officials from protesting the raiding of their teams by the British, whose task became grooming homegrown talent. As the 1936 Games approached, the Canadians continued to complain, which threatened the participation of Great Britain in the Olympics. Only when they relented were the British given the green light.

Among those involved in the dispute was goaltender Jimmy Foster, who had played for Canada previously and transferred to England without permission from Canadian hockey authorities as international rules stipulated. Britain threatened to pull out of the Olympics if Foster and forward Alex Archer could not compete, leading to the withdrawal of the Canadian protest. It was a gesture of goodwill they would come to regret.[78]

Olympic hockey in 1936 would hardly be recognized today. Some of the games were held on frozen Lake Riessersee, which had no boards around the sides to stop checked players. The opener pitting Canada and Poland was played in a snowstorm and had to be delayed during one stretch so the puck could be located.

The British team zoomed through the preliminaries with shutouts of Sweden and Japan. But it seemed doomed from the start of the semifinals. The Brits were placed in a division with Canada and host Germany, which did not bode well. And top goal-scorer Gerry Davey, who had been born in Canada before moving to England at age sixteen, had taken ill. Davey forced himself out of bed to join his teammates for a first-round battle against Canada. Nicklin wasted no time sending Davey onto the ice, and the strategy paid off when he blasted a long shot past Canadian goaltender Francis Moore off a faceoff a mere twenty seconds into the game.

Another hero quickly emerged. To the dismay of all involved in Canadian hockey, it was Foster who performed brilliantly throughout the Olympics. He turned away all but one shot against Canada, but his heroics appeared only strong enough most of the game to forge only a tie. Then it happened. With just over one minute remaining, teammate Don Dailley fired a shot that caromed off Moore. Brit Edgar "Chirp" Brenchley chipped the rebound into the net to clinch a stunning victory.

Little could anyone have imagined just how consequential that triumph would become. For another dispute soon arose. Tournament officials announced that the results of that game and all others in the semifinals would count toward the final round. The decision cleared a path for Britain to win the gold medal if they remained unbeaten. The sudden declaration infuriated the Canadians, but there was nothing they could do. It was deemed by their hockey officials and media a "manipulation" and "regrettable." They failed to learn about the system being used until after the defeat to the British. Their appeal was turned down.

The rest was anticlimactic. The two teams would not embark on another showdown in the final round. The red-hot Foster did not allow a goal in the last two games, a 5–0 shellacking of Czechoslovakia and 0–0 tie against the United States. Canada also won both its games, including a 1–0 victory over the Americans. That proved meaningless. The British were given gold greatly as a result of their head-to-head win over Canada in the semis. And the Canadians came to rue the day they relented and allowed the hottest goaltender in international hockey to play for a team that likely would not have captured the Games without him and prevent their own team from snagging their fifth consecutive gold medal.

And it was not even the first triumph for Britain in Germany. That was when they refused to give the Nazi salute during the opening ceremonies. Nine years later, England would put the finishing touches on far more significant battlefields. It was called World War II.

QUESTION 26: WHAT CITIES LOST NHL FRANCHISES?

The list is not as long as one might think. Many teams have moved from one city to another. But the NHL found its way back.

The early days of the league were replete with franchise shifts. And most of the cities that lost clubs soon or eventually thereafter returned hockey to their fans. A few hightailed it out more than once.

Among them was Quebec. The Bulldogs arrived in 1919 and left the following year. The folding of the World Hockey Association placed the Quebec Nordiques into the NHL in 1979. But they moved to Colorado to become the Avalanche sixteen years later.

The Philadelphia Quakers were equally short-lived. They started in 1930 and folded in 1931 with a wretched 4-26-4 record. That horrible mark and the Great Depression combined to doom hockey in Philadelphia until expansion doubled the number of NHL franchises in 1967 and the Flyers began a run of more than a half-century.

Several franchises were destroyed by the Great Depression. Among them was the Pittsburgh Pirates, who played in the league from 1925 to 1930 before leaving to become the Quakers. Another was the Ottawa Senators, who folded in 1934 after seventeen seasons in the NHL. A team with the same nickname arrived again via expansion in 1992.

A similar fate befell the St. Louis Eagles. That club lasted just one year and was gone in 1935. The city with the iconic Gateway Arch also found its way back in the league in 1967 as the Blues.

Two other Midwestern cities were not as fortunate. Kansas City never got a team back after losing the Scouts after two years in 1976. It's no wonder fans didn't show up—they finished their run with an outrageously terrible 27-110-23 record and left to become the Colorado Rockies. The Cleveland Barons fared a bit better on the ice but also bolted in 1978 following two losing seasons to merge with the Minnesota North Stars.

That team left to become the Dallas Stars in 1993. But the hockey hotbed in the Twin Cities was not without major league hockey for long. The expansion Wild joined the NHL in 1997.

Atlanta twice lost franchises. The Flames flamed out after hanging around from 1972 to 1980 and moved to Calgary. The Thrashers made it a bit longer, playing in the NHL from 1999 to 2011 before bolting to Winnipeg to become the Jets. That Canadian city had lost the Jets to Arizona in 1996.

Another victim was Hartford. The Whalers had played in the WHA and landed in the NHL when it folded. They remained in the league from 1979 to 1997, then moved to Carolina as the Hurricanes.

Stability is a key to success of any sports league. The NHL has had less of it than the NFL, MLB, and NBA. Some believe the NHL has bitten off more than it could chew with thirty-two teams across the United States and Canada. The higher number of teams creates a greater threat that at least one or more will fail. But it also increases exposure to a greater area.

QUESTION 27: WHAT IS THE ZAMBONI MACHINE AND HOW DID IT GET ITS NAME?

It is the most famous vehicle in sports outside auto racing. It is an ice-resurfacing machine better known as the Zamboni. And it has been around for more than seventy years.

The basic requirement at hockey arenas was the brainchild of Frank Zamboni, the son of Italian immigrants. He had moved from Utah to Paramount, California, near Los Angeles. The engineer and his brother toiled at an auto repair shop before teaming up on an electric service business that specialized in manufacturing large refrigeration units for the dairy and produce industries. They built a plant that produced block ice used to prevent perishable goods from spoiling while in transport.

In 1939, the brothers took advantage of the growing popularity of figure skating by opening up the Iceland Skating Rink in their hometown. And soon they combined the knowledge gained from their original profession to improve their business and maintain an ideal surface on ice that was being chipped away constantly by nearly a thousand skaters daily.

Walking behind a scraper pulled by a tractor that scooped up the loose ice, spraying the surface with water, and then squeegeeing it proved quite labor and time intensive. It took more than an hour. So, Frank Zamboni went to work. He built the first machine called a Model A resurfacer out of war surplus parts. It featured a hydraulic changer from a bomber. The invention has changed little since he received a patent in 1949.

The Zamboni has required improvement. It travels slowly on the rink, its sharp blades shaving a thin layer of ice while a rotating horizontal auger collects what has been loosened and places it into a snow collection tank. The machine releases water from the back to clean the ice before it is collected by a squeegee, then vacuumed, filtered, and returned to the tank. Clean water from a separate tank is then sprayed onto the ice and smoothed with a large towel.

A year after it was invented, this ingenious method caught the attention of the most famous figure skater in the world, Olympic champion Sonja Henie, who ordered two machines for her traveling tour. Chicago Stadium owner Arthur Wirtz, who was responsible for that tour, feared that the Zamboni was so unique and fun to watch doing its job that it would cost him money. "People will stay in the stands and watch it and not go down to the concession stands," he said. Even *Peanuts* creator Charles Schulz weighed in. He wrote a Charlie Brown quote claiming that the Zamboni resurfacing the ice was one of three things people love to stare at, the other two being a crackling fire and a flowing stream.[79]

Word of the magic machine spread. The Boston Bruins became the first NHL team to use it in 1954. The five other organizations eventually noticed its effectiveness in smoothing the ice and saving valuable time and energy. The Zamboni became a mainstay in league arenas and was used at the 1960 Winter Olympics in Squaw Valley, California. A decade later the growing number of baseball and football stadiums with artificial surfaces rather than natural grass required what became known as Astro Zambonis to keep surfaces slicked by rain playable. Fred Zamboni even created two other machines: one that helped roll and unroll the turf and another that removed its paint.

By 2015, the Zamboni Company had manufactured about ten thousand machines and were producing around two hundred a year. Competitors came and went, though the Resurface Corporation of Ontario, Canada, earned some lasting success by adding NHL clients and landing the contract for the 2010 Winter Games. But embarrassment resulted when their electric machines failed to properly clean the ice during the men's five-hundred-meter speedskating event to cause a long delay.

Zambonis have become so legendary in hockey circles and beyond that even its drivers have gained fame. The most notable is Al Sabotka, who was forced for years to not only scoop up loose ice as he maneuvered the machine around the ice at Detroit Red Wings games but also clean up thrown octopuses as well. The clever marketing people at Zamboni even launched a "Driver of the Year" campaign in 1999 to celebrate the fiftieth anniversary of the one-of-a-kind machine. The honor was given to Jimmy Macneil, who had for years driven it in Brantford, Ontario, the hometown of scoring whiz Wayne Gretzky. Macneil received the thrill of cleaning the ice at the All-Star Game that year in Toronto. He had the time of his life. "It's a thrill right up there with getting married and having children," he exclaimed.

The Zamboni has made its way into modern pop culture. A rogue Zamboni killed off Eddie LeBec (played by Jay Thomas), the love interest of Carla (played by Rhea Perlman) on the legendary sitcom *Cheers*. Thomas was being considered for a permanent role on the show, but his nasty comment on a radio program about the difficulty of pretending to be sexually interested in Carla angered Perlman, who demanded that he not only leave the show but be killed off.[80]

The machine has also been involved in real-life humor. Two employees at a Boise, Idaho, staking rink were fired after maneuvering a Zamboni through a Burger King drive-thru in 2006.

Few products of any kind in world history were invented at such a perfect level that they never required improvement. The Zamboni is among them. And for many reasons, including the fun name and the job required, it has grown into one of the most beloved and iconic machines of all time.

QUESTION 28: HOW HAS THE NHL POINT SYSTEM CHANGED OVER THE YEARS?

One goal of every sports league is to reward regular-season excellence. Though one and all yearn to include a lot of teams in the playoffs so fans in as many cities as possible can experience post-season runs, they also prefer not to cheapen the regular season by rewarding clubs with losing records. The possibility of a .500 or worse team taking home a title is embarrassing.

Half of the NHL teams qualify for the playoffs. But those that perform the best during the regular season have generally ended the year skating around with the Stanley Cup. Its point system has changed over the years, but the goal has remained the same and has for the most part been achieved. One example is the 2021–2022 season. Every team that reached the playoffs finished at least fifteen games over the break-even mark.

The unique point system embraced by the NHL lasted from its beginning in 1917 through the 1982–1983 season. It awarded two points to winning teams, one for a tie, and zero for a defeat. And when the third period was over, so was the game.

That last rule did not jive with those of the other major sports. By that time, the NFL had for nine years played overtime in its quest to finish games with a winner. The MLB and NBA had never concluded contests in a tie. So, the NHL decided to add an extra session as well in 1983.

That was a throwback to the early days of the league. Teams did play in overtime to determine a winner from 1917 to 1942 (though it was shortened from twenty minutes to ten in 1928). But train-scheduling restrictions during World War II motivated the

NHL to discontinue it so players could get to their next destinations on time. It was never inspired to reinstate overtime over the next four decades.

Teams wasted no time launching the new rule in 1983. Two overtime games were played in their openers on October 5. Neither concluded with a winner. Neither the Minnesota North Stars nor Los Angeles Kings could unknot a 3–3 tie while the Detroit Red Wings and Winnipeg Jets finished at 6–6. The first NHL player in the new era to score an overtime goal was Bob Bourne, who lit the lamp four days later for the New York Islanders in an 8–7 defeat of the Washington Capitals.

The institution of an overtime session did not alter the NHL point system. It simply resulted in fewer ties. But another change that created more excitement eliminated ties. And that was the shootout—yet another wrinkle placed into the rulebook in 2005 after the lost lockout season. Hockey purists railed against it, calling it a gimmick and a bastardization of the sport. But it brought an added sense of drama for fans.

The rules of the shootout are a bit more extensive than some might understand. It begins if neither team scores in the five-minute overtime. Each team then receives three "penalty shots." They are akin to breakaways that goaltenders must try to stop. If one team scores on the first two and the other team fails to score, the game is over.

Sometimes it does not end there. If both teams score the same number of goals on the penalty shots, they send their best shootout artist onto the ice for another attempt. If the player scores, the opposition must score on its try to keep the game going. If both players miss the shootout, it extends into yet another round. That process continues until a winner can be declared.

Shootout winners receive the usual two points in the standings. But the losing team is rewarded one point for forcing a shootout.

Those who voiced opposition to the shootout received a bit of a break when the NHL deemed the number of points teams earned on regulation and overtime victories the first tiebreaker in playoff seeding. But that did not placate critics. Included among them was hockey writer Stu Hackel, who offered the following about what he termed the "postgame skills competition: "I have always found [it] a contrived way to arrive at a result. It's deciding the outcome of a hockey game without actually playing hockey and I want to see hockey. Sudden-death overtime is one big reason why Stanley Cup play is the best hockey of the year. I'll take more of that."[81]

Indeed, the NHL recognized it as a bit of a gimmick when it ruled that the shootout would not be used in the playoffs. But the excitement it has generated among fans since it was implemented in 2005 has justified its continued use.

QUESTION 29: WHICH NHL DEFENSEMAN CHANGED THE GAME AS A PROLIFIC SCORER?

When the last puck had been slapped in 1967, Doug Mohns of the Chicago Black Hawks had established a single-season NHL record for defensemen by scoring sixty points. He had twenty-five goals and thirty-five assists. It was eye-opening at the time.

But it was nothing—at least compared to what was on the horizon. For a kid named Bobby Orr was soon to make his debut with the Boston Bruins. He would revolutionize the position and remain to many the greatest player who ever laced on a pair of skates, at least until Wayne Gretzky came along.

Orr smashed Mohns's record in his third season in a mere sixty-seven games by leading all defensemen with fifty-five points. His defensive prowess was not overlooked either. Orr won his second consecutive Norris Trophy that year as the top defender in the NHL. But he was merely warming up. He exploded for a league-leading 87 assists and 120 points in the 1969–1970 season to nearly double the previous mark for defensemen. It was a ridiculous total given the previous assumed role of the position to stay back and let the forwards take care of the offense.

It was no anomaly. Orr led the league in assists in five of six years and points overall in 1974–1975. He averaged 122 points per season during that stretch and captured the Norris Trophy in all of them while snagging the Hart Trophy every year from 1970 to 1972. He was the first to ever win three consecutive NHL Most Valuable Player awards.

Orr radically altered not only how defensemen could play but to some extent the game of hockey itself. He introduced a far more aggressive style by rushing the puck up the ice to score or directly set teammates up for shots and goals. "He changed the sport by redefining the parameters of his position," wrote E. M. Swift in *Sports Illustrated*. "A defenseman, as interpreted by Orr, became both a defender and an aggressor, both a protector and a producer. Orr was more than an opportunist. He created opportunities."[82]

Indeed, he created more opportunities for other defensemen to mimic his style and become offensive threats as well. The first was Denis Potvin of the New York Islanders, who averaged ninety points a season from 1974 to 1979. Edmonton Oilers defenseman Paul Coffey and Ray Bourque, who followed Orr in Boston, followed suit.

But none could match Orr in offensive firepower. He could rush the full length of the ice with his speed and puck-handling for assists and goals off sizzling, pinpoint shots. He played with a fiery abandon but always under control. He was the Bruin quarterback on the ice. He dove to block shots and played with both toughness and fluidity.

That Orr would revolutionize the game was a surprise even though when he entered the league at age eighteen no defenseman had scored twenty goals in more than two decades. And no defensemen had ever led the league in assists—he did it five times. When Harry Howell of the New York Rangers won the Norris Trophy in 1967, he turned the honor into a figurative nod to Orr. "I'm glad I won it now because it's going to belong to Orr from now on," he said.[83] Howell was right. Only a series of knee surgeries prevented Orr from dominating for more than a decade.

Orr nearly lost his life immediately after his birth on March 20, 1948, in Parry Sound, Ontario. But his illness waned, and he was fine the next morning. He came from an athletic family. His grandfather played professional soccer in Ireland. His dad turned down a hockey contract with a Boston farm club during World War II to join the Royal Canadian Navy.

Pop wasted no time grooming his son on the ice. The younger Orr began skating at age four and launched his organized hockey career a year later. By age twelve, at 5'2" and 110 pounds, he had already been scouted as a potential pro. He signed a contract with the Bruins at a mere fourteen years old with the agreement that he would live at home and commute three hours to games. Orr competed against junior hockey players six years his senior. By the time he was sixteen, his image was splashed on the cover of Canadian magazine *Maclean's*. It was a remarkable rise.

Orr gained a keen awareness of the business of hockey. Well before the advent of free agency and athletic freedom in the major sports he hired attorney Alan Eagleson to represent him. Eagleson negotiated for the eighteen-year-old a then-hefty two-year contract of $50,000 with a $25,000 bonus. It was, at the time, the largest NHL rookie contract ever signed. The well-earned publicity he had already received made him a star before he began gracing the ice at the iconic Boston Garden. It came as no surprise when after scoring thirteen goals he earned Rookie of the Year honors. It also came as no surprise when Boston failed for the eighth consecutive season to reach the playoffs.

Orr would change that too. He transformed the Bruins into a winning team. He finally led them into the postseason in 1968 despite a knee injury and to a Stanley Cup championship in 1970, the year he won all four major awards, including the Conn Smythe Trophy as the playoff MVP. He again spearheaded the club to the crown in 1972. That would remain their last championship until 2011.

"Bobby Orr had the greatest impact of any player to come along in my lifetime," said Canadiens legend and NHL Hall of Famer Jean Beliveau. "He earned his place in hockey history by single-handedly changing the game from the style played in my day to the one we see today. In my mind, there can be no greater legacy."[84]

Orr finished his career with the Black Hawks in 1978. Surgeries had reduced him to a shadow of his former self, but nothing could mar his impact on hockey and legendary status. He had changed the game forever. But though he had opened the sport up for offensive defensemen, nobody has since done it better.

QUESTION 30: WHAT IS CONSIDERED THE MOST HEATED NHL RIVALRY?

It almost doesn't matter the sport. The most intense rivalry will involve a Boston team. Baseball? Yankees-Red Sox. Basketball? Lakers-Celtics. Football? Okay, maybe not. That's probably Packers-Bears. But when Tom Brady was flinging the pigskin and racking up Super Bowl victories, nearly every fan outside New England hated the Patriots.

And hockey? One might think that the mother of all rivalries would be Montreal-Toronto. The sport is king in Canada, so the two oldest franchises in that country must fight the fiercest and most intense battles. Right?

Wrong. The king of all combatants are Montreal and Boston. After all, the Bruins were the first American club in the NHL. They joined in 1924—not long after the Maple Leafs. They had plenty of time to forge the most passionate rivalry with the most successful franchise in professional hockey.

The birth and continuation of the most bitter competition in the league has occurred during the playoffs—regular season games never compare in intensity. The hatred began and strengthened on the Boston side over decades of frustration and defeat—just as it did for the Red Sox during the Yankees dynasty. The Bruins lost a mind-boggling eighteen consecutive series against Montreal from 1947 to 1987. That's quite amazing given that Bobby Orr and his friends won two Stanley Cup titles in the 1970s. They still lost to the Canadiens four times in that decade, including twice in the finals. Montreal even swept Boston four straight in 1977.

The Bruins thereafter exacted at least a bit of revenge. They won four series in a row against the Canadiens from 1990 to 1994. But that was a historically small consolation. Montreal won six Stanley Cup championships at the expense of the Bruins. Boston never captured one against the Canadiens and never will unless an altered divisional setup places them in separate conferences.

The rivalry, however, is not simply based on past results, despite the more than nine hundred meetings between the two franchises. It has intensified by moments in time. Among them was a tie in the seventh and deciding game in the 1952 Stanley Cup semifinals when Canadiens legend Maurice "the Rocket" Richard was hit in the chest and took a stick to the face while trying to split two Boston defenders. His head bounced off the knee of a Bruins player, then his head hit the ice and he was rendered unconscious. The plucky Richard returned to the ice bloodied and bandaged and beat goaltender "Sugar" Jim Henry on a shot to clinch the victory.

Richard was also front and center on March 13, 1955, when he tried to fight Boston's Hal Laycoe and then socked a linesman who attempted to restrain him. Richard was suspended for the rest of the regular season and playoffs. So incensed were fans at the severity of the penalty that they rioted two nights later during a game against Detroit, which eventually beat Montreal in a seven-game Stanley Cup final. A riot ensued in the streets of Montreal in the immediate aftermath of the incident by Canadiens fans that caused extensive damage and even involved an exploding canister of tear gas.

Boston frustration reached a peak in the 1971 quarterfinals. The top-seeded Bruins, who finished the regular season with a sterling 57-14-7 record, led 5-1 in Game 2 before the Canadiens stormed back for a 7–5 win. Boston recovered to take a 3–2 lead in the series but fell apart thereafter on both ends of the ice and lost in seven games.

The beat went on. The archrivals met again in a do-or-die Game 7 in the 1979 semifinals. The Bruins led 4–3 in the third quarter and were two minutes from victory. But they were called for having too many men on the ice, providing the Canadiens with a power play opportunity. Eventual Hall of Famer Guy Lafleur took advantage with the tying goal. To Bruins fans, it seemed like a fait accompli. And sure enough, Montreal's Yvon Lambert tallied the winning goal in overtime. His team went on to beat the New York Rangers for the championship.

As is true with all the most intense rivalries in sport, fans of both cities developed false stereotypical notions of the style of play of their teams and opposition. Offered *Hockey News* and Sportsnet writer Ryan Dixon:

> A certain frustration-fueled animosity helped give life to the New Englanders' notion that Montreal might win the games, but the real men could be found in black and gold, hiding from nothing and punching anything. The counter-perspective in Quebec was that skill won the day over goonery, giving every fan of what really counts in hockey reason to be happy. Bostonians seethed over a mug of suds; Montrealers celebrated with a glass of *rouge*.[85]

No sports domination lasts forever. Just as the Red Sox flipped the script against the Yankees in 2004 and beyond, so did the Bruins fifteen years earlier when they finally beat the Canadiens in the playoffs. Boston took the next three series against Montreal as well, including a four-game sweep in 1992.

That the Bruins, who lost the next three matchups between the two teams, might never catch up in overall postseason competition is not consequential to the past and future of hockey. What does matter is the rivalry itself. All sports leagues need a few heated ones to maximize their appeal.

The NHL features several that are either based on geographical proximity or intense playoff clashes. Included among them are the Canadiens-Maple Leafs, Penguins-Capitals, and Devils-Rangers. But none has reached the level of passion for both fans and players than that between Boston and Montreal.

QUESTION 31: WHY DO HOCKEY PLAYERS LOSE THEIR TEETH?

A typical reply from someone who knows little about the sport when asked about hockey players is that they often have teeth missing. Other impressions come to mind immediately from knowledgeable fans, but those ignorant about the game are right. Many who spend time bashing foes into the boards and colliding with them on the ice do lose the old Chiclets on occasion.

There are many reasons for this. Perhaps the most important in the modern era is that some players refuse to protect their teeth by wearing caged helmets. Some do not like how the helmets feel on their heads and claim that they negatively impact their performance. Others simply go cage-free out of a sense of machismo. They even take pride in losing teeth and consider it a badge of honor. Young players see it as a rite of passage.

And it happens. Hockey players with no protection are sometimes hit in the face by sticks wielded by defenders while passing or striking the puck. They might be wearing a mouth guard, but that only protects the front teeth.

Those who believe hockey is merely a contact sport have never watched it at the highest levels. It is a collision sport much like football but with long, solid sticks, flying pucks, and players moving at much faster speeds. All NFL players are required to wear helmets designed to prevent head trauma and keep their teeth in place. Such is not the case in the NHL.

Jarring a tooth or two loose can happen in a myriad of ways. It can occur when players are bunched near the goalpost and one is hit in the face with a stick or rebounding puck.

Even a mouth guard is not a given. Most players do not wear one. The NHL Players Association negotiated a contract that stipulates its use as a personal choice. Some players claim wearing one makes it more difficult to breathe, particularly if attached to a face mask. And the knowledge that hockey players can have their teeth jarred loose despite the mouth guard motivates many to disregard the option. What some also disregard is that the mouth guard does not only protect the teeth. It also protects the jaw and can prevent concussions, although not completely.

Veteran hockey players have plenty of experience trying to avoid falls and absorbing blows that can cause injury. But sometimes they do not have the time to get out of the way. An elbow or puck moving one hundred miles per hour or faster to the mouth can knock out teeth even if they are wearing a mouth guard. Controlling movement in hockey is harder than it is in other sports simply because it is played on ice.

The loss of teeth can easily be avoided by wearing a face shield. But a perceived weakening of effectiveness based on a lack of visual sharpness, a sense of machismo, and a hockey tradition have all contributed to a refusal of some players to protect themselves. The result is that players who have little or no excuse for getting their teeth knocked out still get their teeth knocked out.

QUESTION 32: WHAT DO REFEREES AND LINESMEN DO?

In basketball and football, there are referees. In baseball, they are called umpires. Only in hockey among the major sports do officials have two different titles. There are two referees and two linesmen.

Both have their own set of responsibilities. Referees are in charge of calling goals and penalties. The primary duty of linesmen is to call offsides and icing. Both wear pinstriped jerseys and black pants. But referees distinguish themselves by wearing orange armbands on both sleeves.

That was not always the setup in the NHL. The league originally used a two-official system that featured one referee and one linesman. That lasted nearly two decades until the 1933–1934 season when it added a referee for five years before reverting back to its original configuration.

The NHL tinkered again in 1941. It implemented a one-referee, two-linesmen arrangement that was not altered until 1998. That is when it experimented with four officials of two referees and two linesmen for twenty games per team. It was expanded to twenty-five games the following season and became permanent in 2000. The motivation for adding officials was to ease their workload and provide another set of eyes on the action of players who had become bigger, stronger, and faster over the years.

It had become apparent that one referee could not see and call every infraction, particularly those that occurred behind the play he was viewing. One referee simply could not keep up given their responsibility for calling goals on both sides of the ice. That gave them too much territory to cover.

Two referees cover more ice. The lead ref is generally stationed in the corner along the goal line while the trail partner is positioned in the neutral zone. They switch roles when play transitions to the other end of the rink. That way two are always covering the action end of the ice.

The system is not perfect. A game with twelve players (five skaters and two goaltenders per side) and four officials causes overcrowding. The referees and linesmen sometimes get in the way. They can inadvertently interfere with the players and puck. That usually has no negative impact on the game. But the officials have either prevented or caused goals. If a puck deflects off an official and into the net, it is waved off. But one can never know if the score would have happened anyway.

Hockey officials are no different from their peers in other sports. They blow calls. They make mistakes. Their jobs are difficult given the pace of play and substantial area of the ice to cover. Some blow whistles more frequently than others. Yet few have complained. The league and its players seem to agree that the advantages of the two-referee setup have proven to outweigh the disadvantages though despite occasional discussions on the ice no official can overrule another.

The on-ice officials are not alone in making certain all runs smoothly. Others officiate off the ice. One judge sits between each goal and helps confirm scores. Their views can be overruled by referees. Video judges are called upon when goals are difficult to determine or have been disputed. They can override a referee ruling. Games also feature an official scorer to keep records of the penalties, goals, and assists; a penalty time-keeper to ensure that those in the box serve the allotted time; and a game time-keeper to start and stop the clock and announce when a period is nearly over.

There were no female officials through the 2021–2022 season, though their inclusion in NHL games seems inevitable. Several are rising through the ranks and have refereed international and minor league games. Given the influx of female officials in the NFL and NBA, one expects the NHL to give the green light within a few years.

QUESTION 33: WHY ARE THERE FEWER FIGHTS IN HOCKEY IN THE 2000S?

Times have changed. Tastes have changed. Fanbases that once drooled over fisticuffs in NHL games in the twentieth century and even beyond began to thirst for clean contests in more recent years. They have grown more sophisticated. Though some continued to tune in to games on TV or show up in person to watch combatants duke it out, studies showed that the majority preferred fight-free battles on the ice.

Statistics indicated during that time frame the same trend among players. The number of fights plummeted through the course of the early 2000s. By the end of its second decade, the number had fallen to less than one every five games, whereas ten years earlier it was more than one fight every two games. And though the number rose a bit in 2020, it had become apparent that it would never again rise to previous levels. Neither the league nor the players and fans advocated for or desired a return to the bad old days that featured "goons" and enforcers on the ice for short periods to wreak havoc.

But fights in the NHL rarely escalate into brawls. Rules both written and unwritten allow them to occur but regulate their length and intensity to prevent serious injury. Among those guidelines is that players drop their gloves before letting loose. That gives both parties the time to realize that the fight is on so one cannot start it by jumping on the other.

Some NHL players in more recent years have simply started skating away. That is considered by others bad form. One such instance occurred in a game between Washington and Boston in 2019 during which Bruins forward Brad Marchand exchanged shoves with Capitals center Lars Eller. Eller dropped a glove and prevented Marchand from leaving the scene by grabbing his collar and continued to hold on when the linesmen stepped in to separate them. Eller was forced to let go and complained about it after the game.

"I would rather fight him but can't fight a guy that doesn't want to fight," Eller said. "Everybody saw what he is . . . I don't think there's a lot of integrity in his game."[86]

That any player is chastised by a peer for refusing to fight suggests the league has a long way to go to eliminate fighting if it so desires. But Eller was also motivated by an incident on opening night when Marchand was the aggressor and the former felt he had been jumped. Marchand was motivated on the first occasion by Eller celebrating a goal in a 7–0 slaughter. That history between the two indicated that Marchand broke hockey etiquette by not engaging, never mind that his inaction resulted in a minor penalty for Eller and power play for his team.

The reasons for fighting in hockey run deep and have changed over time. It is far from mindless brawling. Whereas once enforcers were deemed necessary and allowed to play a few minutes here and there over those with greater offensive and defensive skills, they have more recently faded from the scene. The motives have become more nuanced but often revolve around protecting teammates whom players believe have been perceived as victimized by dirty play by an opponent on the ice. Fighting is therefore sometimes deemed necessary in a collision sport.

And though the goons and enforcers are gone, players know about their teammates and from surveying opposing rosters who is willing and even eager to drop gloves and fight. That is the understanding throughout the league. They pick and choose targets often based on value.

"I try and really make sure the guys nowadays that I'm fighting have a role on the other team, that they're out there playing minutes," said Capitals winger Tom Wilson. "There's still guys like that around the league that are big parts of their teams that are willing to fight. If you get a five-minute major, you could be in the box for 10 minutes because you have to wait for a whistle. It can be a huge chunk of time so you've got to be really smart about it."

That mentality reflects a change from the past in modern hockey dictating choice. The general consensus became that players should be free to avoid fighting if they prefer. That is certainly true in regard to instigating fights. Officials levy stiffer penalties on aggressors. In 1992, the NHL altered its rule on instigating a fight to make the punishment a game misconduct. Four years later, the league further mandated that aggressors can be given a two-minute minor, five-minute major, and a ten-minute misconduct penalty.

Refusing to fight, however, can be risky. Those who refuse to retaliate by throwing down their gloves might place their teammates in danger. They could simply be targeted instead by a player seeking to protect his own teammate after a perceived dirty hit.

Fighting has certainly become less a part of hockey, which most agree is a positive direction for the sport. The written and unwritten rules that govern it prove it remains alive. But they also seek to avoid fighting. Players dropping gloves and going at it mano a mano has never been a major problem. When fights escalate into brawls by people wielding sticks, they become dangerous. But when people wielding sticks during game action show they want to use them on opponents beyond the rules of the game, fighting becomes a necessary component of the sport and can prevent battles on the ice from getting out of hand.

QUESTION 34: WHAT IS A "ONE-TIMER" IN HOCKEY?

No, this is not a guy person plays one game or one season in the NHL. It is a shot—usually a slapshot—taken directly off a pass without stopping the puck. It requires a quick release and is used to surprise a goaltender or give him little time to react.

It is called a one-timer because it is a do-or-die shot. If a shooter does not make a solid connection or aim the puck properly, the chance of scoring is gone. It is a quick-release, one-time opportunity. They must be struck with speed and power. But when executed well, it is extremely difficult to defend.

Not all hockey players can pull it off effectively. It takes extensive practice. One must time it so the stick hits the ice simultaneously with the arrival of the puck. Players must be adept not only at slapshots but also at aiming the puck for areas of the net that make it tough for goaltenders to complete a save.

One-timers are indeed generally performed taking slapshots. That is when the stick is raised high, which gives the shot more pace but a more difficult wrinkle to the timing of the shot in one smooth motion. There must be no delay from the end of the backswing to the completion of the one-timer shot or it invariably fails.

It can also be important to strike when the goaltender is moving. That happens often when they have just made a save. One-timer shots with short or no backswings, such as when a player flips the puck toward an open area of the net, can best be achieved before a goalie gets resettled following a save and does not have the time to react to another shot.

The effectiveness of a one-timer results from three basic advantages sought out by the shooter. One is the angle from the goal between the pass and shot based on goaltender positioning. A poor, wide angle gives any shot little chance of success. Another is the change of direction of the puck. A one-timer executed with speed and precision gives goalies little time to react to that change of direction. The third is simply speed. One-timers struck with maximum power also minimizes save possibilities. One-timers simply create higher success rates than a one-on-one shot between shooter and goalie.

Given the trickiness of pulling off a one-timer successfully, it is no wonder that those who have gained the greatest success in doing so over the years reads like an NHL who's who of offensive juggernauts. Prolific scorers such as Brett Hull and Wayne Gretzky—the Great One—could match one-timers with the best of them. But in more modern times, Washington Capitals superstar Alex Ovechkin and Tampa Bay Lightning all-star Steve Stamkos have generally been considered the premier one-timers.

QUESTION 35: WHO WERE THE GREATEST OLYMPIC PLAYERS EVER?

There is too much subjectivity here to answer definitively. But one cannot go wrong starting with Finnish scoring machine Teemu Selanne and Russian goaltender Vladislav Tretiak.

Selanne remained through 2022 the only hockey player to compete in six different Winter Olympics—each one from 1992 to 2014. He holds the record with thirty-seven games played. But that statistic alone is merely the tip of the iceberg. He owns a slew of Olympic records, including his forty-three points (twenty-four goals and nineteen assists). Though his teams never won a goal medal, they did garner one silver and three bronze.

Selanne also exhibited his vast talents for several NHL teams during that same period, including the Winnipeg Jets, Anaheim Mighty Ducks, and San Jose Sharks. He played one of the longest stretches in league history and earned four all-star nods.

Tretiak never set skate on NHL ice due to Cold War era restrictions in the Soviet Union, but he certainly made his mark on the international stage and is considered by some as the greatest goaltender in history. He starred in every Olympiad from 1972 to 1984 and played critical roles in his team winning three gold medals. His team won sixteen games with him between the pipes—an Olympic record. He allowed a mere 1.92 goals per game.

Another standout from an Eastern Bloc country under Soviet influence who therefore never received a shot at the NHL was Czechoslovakian Vlastimil Bubnik, who participated in each Games from 1952 to 1964. Though his teams did not manage to medal until placing third in the last, one could not put the blame on

Bubnik. He did his part, scoring twenty-two goals and adding fifteen assists in just twenty-eight games. Bubnik was a sensationally versatile athlete. He even scored four goals on the soccer fields in international competition.

A Czech superstar fortunate enough to compete in the post–Cold War era was goaltender Dominik Hasek, who played for his native country in the Olympics in 1988, 1998, 2002, and 2006. His teams won five of six games in 1998 to earn the gold medal. He posted an outrageous 0.97 goals against average that year while saving more than 96 percent of shots on goal. Hasek wasted little time taking his talents into the NHL and eventually emerging as a superstar with the Buffalo Sabres. He won six Vezina Trophies as the top goaltender in the league.

The best scoring defenseman in Olympic hockey history was Soviet star Viacheslav Fetisov, who competed in 1980, 1984, and 1988. He belied the typical objective of his position by racking up twelve goals and twenty-one assists. His talents played a key role in the Russians earning two consecutive gold medals after the stunning upset defeat to the United States in 1980. Fetisov even coached the Soviets to a bronze medal in 2002.

Easily the most prolific scorer in Olympic history was Canadian Harry Watson. The show he put on in 1924 proved mind-boggling. His team played only five times, but he recorded an absurd thirty-seven goals and nine assists—an average of 9.2 points per game. The rules of the game at the time helped Watson (there were nearly twenty goals scored per game during the event), but his achievement should not be underappreciated. It was no wonder the Canadians cruised to the gold medal that year. But Watson did not only shine as an Olympian. His tremendous NHL career, mostly with the Toronto Maple Leafs, earned him a spot in the Hockey Hall of Fame.

Swedish goaltender Henrik Lundqvist ranked second all-time through 2022 with twelve Olympic victories. He peaked in the gold-medal performance of his country in 2006, winning five games and allowing just twelve goals. He led his team back to the gold-medal game in 2014 before falling to Canada. He gained greater notoriety as a New York Rangers superstar for fifteen seasons, earning Rookie of the Year honors in 2006 and two All-Star Game appearances.

Perhaps the greatest German hockey star ever was Dieter Hegen. He played in all five Winter Olympics from 1984 to 1998. His name became lost in history because his teams never earned a place on the podium. Despite opponents keying their defenses to stop the left winger, he still managed to score sixteen goals and add seven assists in thirty games. His talents motivated the Montreal Canadiens to draft him in 1981, but he never signed a contract.

One explosive scorer who did star in the NHL was Czech superstar Jaromir Jagr, one of a few players who competed in five Olympiads. His talents helped the first of those squads in 1998 take a gold medal. The lack of talent surrounding him prevented him from a repeat over his last four Games, but he remained a huge offensive threat. Jagr recorded nine goals and fourteen assists in twenty-eight games during his Olympic career. But it was his brilliance mostly with the Pittsburgh Penguins of the NHL that gained him fame in North America. He led the league in points scored five times and was voted an all-star eight times, including every year from 1995 to 2001.

Perhaps the player who forged the most interesting Olympic career was Czechoslovakian Peter Stastny, who played for that country in 1980, and then after the fall of Communism represented the nation of Slovakia fourteen years later. Though neither team earned a medal, he dominated with twelve goals and eleven assists in just fourteen games. He was particularly efficient in 1980, with seven goals and seven assists. Like many other players given an opportunity to make big bucks and gain greater fame in the NHL,

Stastny took full advantage. He became one of the top scorers in that league with the Quebec Nordiques from 1980 to 1989 before finishing his career with New Jersey and St. Louis.

The number of Olympic standouts over a century of competition runs well into the hundreds. But the best of the best made the most memorable contributions, whether their teams earned opportunities to stand on the podium for medal ceremonies or not.

QUESTION 36: WHY DO GOALIES "SCRAP" SKATES ON THE CREASE BEFORE EACH PERIOD?

Goaltenders do not like Zambonis. The goal of the machine is to make the ice as slippery as possible. Goalies prefer pucks that do not travel so fast. So, they employ a little housekeeping in front of their nets before every period, including before a game. They will scrape the ice to remove that slipperiness and make it harder for the puck to slide. Goaltenders also seek to smooth out the area to create a more even surface and controllable puck.

Forwards and defensemen appreciate the work done by Zambonis. They prefer maximum slipperiness for skating. But goalies want to slow the puck down. They are not allowed to build up a pile of snow in front of their hockey homes—crews arrive on the scene to remove any excess—but they certainly use the scraping technique to help maximize their effectiveness. Some goals fly through the air, but many others slide in along the ice or even trickle in. Goaltenders cannot be blamed for working to slow them down.

Another reason goaltenders prefer the ice around the crease is their own mobility. They continually move back and forth and slide from post to post while their teammates work to prevent clear shots. Control of body movements can be critical and the difference between a save and a goal. Goalies do not want to over-slide on slippery ice. Making saves is all about quick positioning.

That takes extensive practice, even before games when teammates pepper goalies with shots. Working the crease in front of the net allows goaltenders to prepare their bodies, particularly their legs, to get a feel for the edges of their skates and focus on the task ahead. What is known as scrapping can prove beneficial to both the mental and physical state.

And even the Zamboni is not infallible. Sometimes it can leave bumps on the ice near the goal that goaltenders must smooth out. Even the slightest bump can change the trajectory of a shot, which could cost a save and even a close game. A Zamboni also cannot prevent snow from piling up in and around the crease during play. That allows goalies to sneak some of the excess to the sides of the goals to prevent players from wrapping the puck into the net from behind. They are in a constant battle with maintenance crews that skate on the ice to shovel off snow. Call it the game within the game.

QUESTION 37: HOW LONG DO HOCKEY GAMES LAST?

The length of contests in every major sport but baseball is dictated greatly by a game clock. Such is the case in hockey. But the allotted times for each period are not the same at various levels. Stoppages of play such as for penalties and sometimes overtime alter the minutes required from initial faceoff to the final buzzer.

Hockey games in the NHL and internationally both feature three periods of twenty minutes each. Intermissions in both run fifteen minutes, though several hockey websites claim play stops seventeen or eighteen minutes in the NHL for televised contests. The average time it takes to complete an NHL game is usually around two hours and twenty minutes.

Interestingly, given the increased amount of time it has taken to complete baseball and football games in recent years, the average length of NHL games has actually decreased a bit during the course of the twenty-first century. But depending on commercial time, penalties, injuries, fights, overtime, and other factors, they can still last up to three hours.

At those higher levels of the sport, including the American Hockey League, juniors, and premier youth leagues, the game clock stops with every whistle for infractions. That is not necessarily the case with recreational hockey. Those games are much shorter due to a running clock. Many of their battles are predetermined to last just one hour, though there are short stoppages between periods. College contests are a bit shorter than professional games. Allotted times for periods, including overtime and intermissions, are the same, but there are most often no commercial interruptions.

Like any sport, inaction takes far longer than action. But there are longer stretches of action in hockey than in any of the other major sports. NBA games feature four twelve-minute quarters for forty-eight minutes total, with frequent interruptions for free throws and timeouts. Activity in football and baseball is far more sporadic. The sixty minutes of action in hockey are mostly continuous, which means that nearly half of the total game time can keep fans on the edge of their seats rather than seeking out hot dog and beer vendors.

Games tied after regulation obviously add length. An overtime in which wins and losses remain undecided run five minutes. Though the loser still receives one point in the standings, a shootout keeps the battle going if the score is still knotted until a winner is determined. Overtime sessions are extended to twenty minutes in the playoffs with no shootouts.

The result historically of preventing ties in the playoffs has led to many marathons over a century of hockey in the NHL. The longest game ever was played between Detroit and Montreal Maroons in the semifinals on March 24, 1936. Game 1 of the eventual Red Wings sweep remained scoreless through five overtimes and extended into a sixth, which ended when rookie Mud Bruneteau finally tallied a goal. He had only scored two goals throughout the regular season. The total game time at the legendary Montreal Forum that day was 116 minutes and 30 seconds.

The other six-overtime game in NHL history had been played three years earlier in the semifinals between Toronto and Boston. It was also in a scoreless battle and was far more dramatic because it was the deciding Game 5. It proved to be the highlight of the short career of Maple Leafs forward Ken Doraty, who scored the only goal. That sent his team into the Stanley Cup finals, where it lost to the New York Rangers.

Modern-era playoff clashes have also lasted deep into the night. The longest was played on May 4, 2000, between Philadelphia and Pittsburgh for a shot at the Eastern Conference finals. The ninety-two-minute Game 4 was clinched for the Flyers on a Keith Primeau goal and proved to be a critical victory in a series won by Philadelphia after the Penguins had forged a 2–0 lead.

All sports pride themselves on drama, especially in regard to overtime. They can all end suddenly and dramatically. That is why the NHL instituted shootouts. Nobody likes a tie. There is a level of satisfying finality when a shootout finally determines a winner. And they have indeed added a level of drama that an overtime tie could never match.

QUESTION 38: WHAT ARE THE MINOR LEAGUES OF HOCKEY?

Times have changed. The American Hockey League housed fewer than ten teams through most of its history. But several events in the sport affecting the NHL and developmental leagues that have come and gone left the AHL as the only one used as a direct player pipeline to the big boys of professional hockey.

What was once known as the International American Hockey League began its affiliation with the NHL in 1936. Since then, it has served a useful purpose. NHL teams have, when needed, constantly pulled players from the I-AHL, which later morphed into the AHL, and sent them back when not. Younger AHL players have been for nearly a century groomed by the NHL for future use.

But whereas once there were once no direct affiliations between specific AHL and NHL franchises, expansion of the former has allowed for such matchups. The modern AHL boasts thirty-two teams—one for each NHL club. Though junior leagues and lower minor leagues such as the East Coast Hockey League (ECHL) also serve to develop players for the big time, the AHL is the only one with direct affiliates to the NHL. The AHL is akin to Triple-A in the MLB, the only league that ranks just one step below. Each team is a farm system for its NHL partner.

The NHL also has an agreement with the Canadian Hockey League, the premier junior circuit in North America. Players under the age of twenty drafted out of that league must be promoted to or loaned back to the NHL since they are not allowed to compete in the league until they leave their teenage years. The only exception is if they have honed their talents in European leagues.

Hockey leagues in America began paying players around the turn of the twentieth century. The practice continued to Canada and throughout the northern part of the United States. The maturation of professional leagues necessitated a developmental system. The need grew particularly pronounced when the Pacific Hockey League folded in 1926 and left many worthy players unemployed. The NHL, which had been in existence less than a decade, took in some of them by expanding from seven teams to ten.

But the burgeoning league still needed places to store and develop all the players too young or not yet skilled enough to earn roster spots. The result was the formation of several minor pro leagues, including the I-AHL, American Hockey Association, and Prairie Hockey League. Soon thereafter, the Pacific Coast Hockey League was born. The I-AHL officially and forever changed its name to the American Hockey League in 1940.

One by one, all but the AHL died. World War II left several hockey league victims, including the PCHL in 1941 and AHA a year later. By the following season there were only twelve teams in the NHL and AHL combined. Players were scattered about fighting overseas or competing in military leagues across North America.

The end of the war returned players back to the ice and resulted in the reformation of old leagues and the creation of new ones. The International Hockley League was launched in 1945, followed by the United States Hockey League a year later and the Pacific Coast Hockey League in 1948.

The IHL proved particularly successful and began battling with the AHL for minor league supremacy. It started with teams only in Detroit and Windsor, Ontario, but by the early 1950s it had become a Midwestern stronghold with clubs in such cities as Flint, Fort Wayne, Muskegon, and Toledo. The IHL gained more franchises when the Central Hockey League folded in 1984, including one as far west as Salt Lake City. But running teams in that league became cost prohibitive as the league landed clubs in major cities, even those with NHL teams such as Chicago and Detroit, as well as Atlanta, Las Vegas, Orlando, and San Francisco.

Not that NHL officials were turning cartwheels over the intrusion. In the 1990s, they began shifting their affiliations away from the IHL, which deprived the latter of the financial backing needed to thrive. The IHL floundered and died in 2001. Its loss was the gain of the AHL, which absorbed the Chicago, Grand Rapids, Houston, Manitoba, Milwaukee, and Utah franchises. Only the representative from the Windy City was housed in an NHL community.

By that time, the ECHL had long been formed. That league was born out of the Atlantic Coast Hockey League, which began operations in 1981 and was quickly established as a developmental circuit for those not drafted by NHL teams. Organizations of that era such as the Sunshine Hockey League Southern Hockey League and Colonial Hockey League, which morphed into the United Hockey League, quickly fell by the wayside.

The ECHL stuck around. By 2003, it had swallowed up the West Coast Hockey League, which had formed in 1995, and the Western Professional Hockey League, born a year later. The ECHL began with five times in four states and eventually expanded to twenty-seven teams in twenty states and two Canadian provinces with more than seven hundred players having played in the NHL. The league developed twenty-seven affiliations with the NHL by 2021. That marked the twenty-fourth consecutive season that the ECHL had at least twenty-four partnerships with NHL franchises.

Many AHL teams are located in the same state as their NHL affiliates, but there are several exceptions. The New York Islanders pluck players from an AHL club in Bridgeport, Connecticut. The Minnesota Wild partner is based in Iowa. The Calgary Flames boast a foreign affiliate in Stockton, California. Other NHL franchises have AHL partners in the same city, including the San Jose Sharks and Toronto Maple Leafs.

The NHL uses two different contracts in its business relationships with AHL talent. A one-way contract results in identical pay no matter which league the player is competing in at a particular time. A two-way contract results in the player being loaned to the AHL but the NHL maintaining responsibility for his salary. It means that the player will receive a higher payment while playing for the NHL. A demotion to the AHL results in a salary drop. An NHL team cannot always call up AHL players.

Some in that minor league are under contract with their club, which must then let a player seeking promotion out of their deal. That setup can certainly prove detrimental to the player, as the average salary was $50,850 in 2021 in the AHL and more than $3 million in the NHL. Though that figure is significantly lower than in MLB, the NFL, and the NBA (greatly due to the struggles of the NHL to land and maintain a national television contract), the difference is huge.

Times have indeed changed not just in skyrocketing incomes but in the comparative lack of competition in minor league hockey. Though a few lower-level leagues continued to form as the twenty-first century rolled along, including the Federal Prospects Hockey League, which was launched in 2010, the AHL and ECHL were the only two significant leagues left standing.

QUESTION 39: WHO ARE THE BEST GOALTENDERS IN NHL HISTORY?

It is impossible in sports to rank the best at any position because the debate is so subjective. But it is easier than ranking those in other professions because one can use statistics as guidelines.

Despite that advantage, the task of listing the premier goaltenders in NHL history cannot be achieved definitively. Goals against averages and save percentages do not provide complete determinations of talent. They are also reflective of teammate effectiveness on defense. Goaltenders play critical roles in winning Stanley Cup championships. Yet even that cannot define greatness. Those who score goals and prevent point-blank shots on their own goalies also earn credit.

Despite the subjectivity of such an undertaking, one can rank as the best of the best for conversation and at least provide some accuracy by studying the numbers and impact on their team and league.

Among those generally considered deserving of the No. 1 spot is Montreal and Colorado legend Patrick Roy, whose greatness keyed the last Canadiens period of glory, including crowns in 1986 and 1993, then took the Avalanche to titles in 1996 and 2001. He paced the league in save percentage four times in five seasons from 1988 to 1992 and twice in goals-against percentage twice during those peak years. The result was six All-Star Game appearances, three Vezina Trophies as the premier goaltender in the NHL, and three Conn Smythe Trophies as the top goalie in the playoffs.

Roy and Boston Bruins counterpart Tony Esposito helped popularize the butterfly style of goaltending introduced more than two decades earlier by Chicago Black Hawks standout Glenn Hall, a positioning of dropping to the knees and spreading the pads to cover the bottom of the net. His brilliance ushered in a new era of modern goaltending and inspired many young players from his native Quebec to alter their desire to become super scorers and instead become goaltenders.

One result of Roy continuing to prove the greater effectiveness of the butterfly position was improved goaltending throughout the league and eventually new rules to increase plummeting scoring totals. Roy was arguably not the finest to ever play the game, but he was the most influential.

Roy, however, does not win the award for style points. Perhaps the most spectacular goaltender to ever don an NHL uniform was Czech import Dominik Hasek, who not only practiced the fundamentals of stopping pucks but also boasted a freakish ability to contort his body to make what seemed like impossible saves.

Hasek played on Buffalo teams with shaky defenses that allowed opponents to pepper one shot after another on goal yet still led the league in save percentage six years in a row. In fact, he paced one and all in number of saves and save percentage at .932 in 1998. Hasek won successive Hart Trophies as league MVP and finished among the top five in voting five times.

His brilliance did not translate into a Stanley Cup championship until he was traded by Buffalo to Detroit during the 2001 offseason and helped the Red Wings win it all that year and in his last season of 2008. He amazingly earned the Jennings Trophy at age forty-three for playing at least twenty-five games for a team with the lowest goals-against average in the league.

One goaltender that must be on any list of the all-time greats launched his NHL career soon after World War II and ended it several years after the Great Expansion despite numbing injuries that would have sidelined most after a few seasons. That was Red Wings legend Terry Sawchuk.

Sawchuk suffered a permanently damaged elbow and sustained more than four hundred stitches to his face, a collapsed lung, broken instep, and severed hand tendons. He left hockey with a curved spine, or lordosis, a condition that prevented him from sleeping more than two hours straight. He also battled alcoholism and depression.

In the context of the problems he faced, the brilliance he displayed on the ice is all the more amazing. He earned four Vezina Trophies and led his teams to four Stanley Cup championships. His 103 career shutouts remained an NHL record until Brodeur broke it in 2009. He sported goals-against averages under 2.0 every year from 1951 to 1955, earning All-Star Game nods in each of them.

Brodeur had long established himself as a Hall of Famer by the time he shattered Sawchuk's shutout mark. His brilliant netminding combined with defensive stalwarts such as Scott Niedermayer transformed the New Jersey Devils into annually one of the toughest team to score against in the NHL. They finished in the top seven in that department every year from 1994 to 2004, ranking first in goals against in 1997, 2003, and 2004. Brodeur won three Stanley Cups during that stretch, peaking when his team snagged the crown and yielded just over two goals per game in 2003.

When Brodeur finally hung up his skates after twenty-two seasons with New Jersey and one short stint with the St. Louis Blues, he owned 691 career wins, 125 shutouts (with an additional 24 in the playoffs), and 28,508 saves, all of which might stand forever as NHL records.

Montreal Canadiens icon Jacques Plante did not merely gain fame for insisting on wearing a mask in 1959 after taking a puck to the face from an Andy Bathgate slapshot. He was an innovator in other aspects of the game, including his straying from his position to support defensemen by playing the puck. He studied opponents with greater scholarship than his contemporaries, jotting down notes about their tendencies and yelling out instructions to teammates based on those inclinations.

Plante backed up his aggressive approach to his job by stopping shots. It's no wonder he won five Vezina Trophies in a row in the 1950s and played critical roles in Montreal claiming the same number of Stanley Cups that decade. Its dynasty of that era could not have been achieved had the Canadiens employed any other goaltender of that period aside from perhaps Glenn Hall. Plante continued to perform well for several teams after leaving Montreal in 1963.

That is when he was traded to the New York Rangers for fellow future Hall of Fame goalie Gump Worsley, who performed well but played more sporadically. By the early 1970s, the Canadiens had unveiled another soon-to-be legend in Ken Dryden. Just months removed from a stint with the AHL Montreal Voyageurs, the rookie broke into the NHL with a bang, winning his first six games with a 1.5 goals-against average. Soon he was helping his team to the 1971 Stanley Cup crown.

The rest is history. But not a long one. Dryden was the most dominant goalie of his era, winning five Vezina Trophies and appearing in six All-Star Games in just eight years. But he was a restless soul. Dryden sat out 1973–1974 season due to a contract dispute, then retired at age thirty-one to explore other avenues for his life after his team had won its fourth consecutive NHL title. He went on to become an author, broadcaster, politician, and Toronto Maple Leafs executive, but not before leading the league in shutouts and wins four times.

Only one goaltender of the 1950s was in the same league—figuratively—with Plante. And that was Hall, who launched his career as a Detroit Red Wings all-star before establishing himself as a Hall of Famer with the Chicago Black Hawks through most of the 1960s. Hall was steady and dependable, leading all NHL goaltenders in games played with seventy every year from 1956 to 1962.

Such faith in Hall would not have been placed by either club had he not performed brilliantly. He earned eleven all-star nods and three Vezina Trophies not just for his dependability but also for his talent. Hall led Chicago to the 1961 Stanley Cup championship. It marked the only time from 1942 to 1969 that the crown was not owned by Montreal, Toronto, or Detroit.

Thirty-six NHL goaltenders grace the Hockey Hall of Fame and one can argue about which of them are the best of the best. But that those listed here are among them cannot be debated.

QUESTION 40: WHO INVENTED THE BUTTERFLY STYLE OF GOALTENDING?

The butterfly method has been described as follows:

> To close off the bottom half of the net by having both knees connect towards the middle of your body while driving them towards the ice. Simultaneously, you are flaring your toes out so your pads continue to face the puck at just the right angle when it's being shot so you are able to direct rebounds towards the corners.[87]

If the achievements of those who launched the use of the butterfly are any indication, it certainly worked from the start. It was pioneered by Black Hawks star and Hall of Famer Glenn Hall. But it was popularized and perfected by Tony Esposito, who followed Hall to Chicago and bucked the establishment by playing with his head below the crossbars. The butterfly forced opponents to lift the puck to get it into the net, which is considered by many to be nearly twice as difficult.

The butterfly was so unaccepted despite Hall's success that Esposito did not land a starting job in the NHL until the age of twenty-six. When he gained stardom, other amateur and professional goalies began to emulate him. "Whenever you played in net in ball hockey, you were always Tony Esposito playing the butterfly," recalled former teammate Steve Larmer.[88]

Given the success of Hall and Esposito, it could be assumed that more goaltenders embraced the style in the 1970s. That would be the wrong assumption. Goaltender coaches railed against it until yet another Hall of Famer adopted it. That was Patrick Roy, who used the butterfly to stop shots blasted along the ice by such prolific scorers as Wayne Gretzky and Mike Bossy. Many of their goals were blasted from beyond the defensive zone faceoff circle. Roy thrived halting the puck using the butterfly style, which also provided an advantage by allowing Roy to use his stick to guide the puck on an angle rather than out in front of him, where rebounds could result in scores. In the modern era, despite the butterfly wreaking havoc on the hips, knees, and back, any other method of goaltending has become archaic.

The popularity of the butterfly was furthered by the use of bigger and more protective padding by goaltenders. The concern in the Esposito era from the late 1960s into the early 1980s was that the butterfly style left openings into which scorers could fire the puck. But larger equipment destroyed any lingering apprehensions, though some "standup" goaltenders try to stay on their feet as much as possible before committing to the butterfly when the threat of a goal arises.

QUESTION 41: WHY ARE THERE SO FEW BLACK PLAYERS IN THE NHL?

The common notion that the large percentage of Black Americans and Black Canadians living in inner cities do not have access to youth hockey in their schools and neighborhoods, nor can they afford expensive equipment, is largely accurate, but it would be wrong to generalize the socioeconomic conditions of the Black community.

The same holds true with baseball, though bats and gloves are far less pricy. The vast majority of Black athletes in the NFL and NBA screams volumes about what sports most of the youth have been playing over several decades.

And though the NHL *talked* a good game about diversity into the 2020s, it has not played one, according to those involved in getting Black youth involved in the sport. Among them are organizations such as Skillz Hockey and the Hockey Diversity Alliance. A request from the latter for NHL financing was rejected.

"[The NHL] has been talking about diversity since '93, but they don't seem to know what to do with this," complained Skillz Hockey founder Kirk Brooks. Added Minnesota Wild defenseman Matt Dumba, a Filipino who founded the Alliance, which he launched after the murder of George Floyd in Minneapolis in 2020, "It just goes back to everything that's been done for a long, long time in the same fashion. You know, the old boys' club and them dictating who is and who isn't welcome. Yeah, I'm sick of it."[89]

Journeyman right wing Anson Carter, a Black player who forged a twelve-year NHL career in the 1990s and 2000s, added that many of his high school friends gave up on the sport for being "too white." But his presence in the league motivated those same buddies to tell him that he inspired their Black kids to take up the sport. "That made me more proud than even playing in the league myself because they're like, 'You played, so why shouldn't my kids play?'" Carter said. "To see that change with the way my friends would think, it's an amazing thing."[90]

The NHL took steps to increase diversity in management within franchises and in the league office. But Kim Davis, who joined the league as executive vice president of social impact, growth, and legislative in 2017, warned against folks expecting too much too soon.

"Anybody that expects us to wave a magic wand and have these things happen immediately as opposed to over time, they don't understand how real change works," Davis said. "What I'm encouraged by is the fact that our owners and our leaders of our 32 clubs and at the NHL level are committed to this. People are leaning into this. They understand that this is, as I often say, a movement not a moment and it's going to take us time to make the change. But we're already seeing it."[91]

In 2022, the NHL boasted fifty-four active players who were Arab, Asian, Black, Latino, or Indigenous, which was just 7 percent of the league. Though that remains far too low in the hearts and minds of many, it represents an increase since Carter last played fifteen years earlier.

Numbers do not tell the whole story. Racism among fans has at times run rampant and has potentially turned off minorities from pursuing a career in the sport as players, coaches, or even front office personnel. One such example occurred in 2018, when Washington Capitals forward Devante Smith-Pelly, who is Black, sat in the penalty box and was taunted by a group of White fans in Chicago chanting "basketball, basketball, basketball" at him. Toronto Maple Leafs Black forward Wayne Simmonds was the victim of an even more disgraceful racial harassment in 2011 when a fan hurled a banana at him during a game. Several other Black players, including K'Andre Miller of the New York Rangers and Nigerian forward Akim Aliu of the Calgary Flames, also reported racist abuse.

The latter detailed problems with his own teammates and coach in the professional ranks in an article he wrote for *The Players' Tribune*. He offered the following about the future of diversity in the league:

> What we can do is promote diversity. I believe that the NHL should adopt something like the Rooney Rule, which requires NFL teams to interview minorities for head coaching and senior football operation positions.
>
> We should be showing off the diversity our game is capable of having. This has an immediate impact on youth involvement. Because I know there are kids like me out there who have a hard time seeing themselves in the NHL. Or there's a little Black boy or girl who wants to be an NHL coach, but he or she doesn't see anyone in the league who looks like them.
>
> I hear the league talk all the time about growing the game by taking it overseas and whatnot. That is great, but I think growing it here at home is just as important. And that international growth is also tied to the fact that there aren't enough personalities in our league. People love soccer and basketball for the characters and stories just as much as for the actual game.
>
> The end goal here is to create a system, from top to bottom, that welcomes and nourishes everyone from every background. There *needs to be*

proper acknowledgment of how diverse our game is becoming. The NHL shoved their LGBTQ and "Hockey is For Everyone" support programs into the same month as Black History Month. When I saw that, it made me feel that people like us, the outcasts, are a chore to them. Something to tick off a checklist and forget about for a year. And when you don't feel like you're encouraged to take part in the game in the sport's *biggest league*, you feel that pain in your soul.[92]

Black players have complained that not enough has changed since Willie O'Ree faced racist taunts after breaking the color barrier in the NHL in 1958 with the Boston Bruins. They have been common in youth hockey and lower professional levels as well.

"[O'Ree] had to go through a lot, and the same thing has been happening now," said Smith-Pelly. "If you had pulled a quote from him back then and us now, they're saying the same thing, so obviously there's still a long way to go in hockey."[93]

Especially for Black Americans. Among the twenty-six Black players on NHL rosters in 2020, only six were from the United States. The rest were Canadian.

QUESTION 42: WHAT ARE ICING AND OFFSIDES?

These are two of the most common infractions in hockey. Neither is considered a penalty, so offenders never serve time in the box for breaking the rules.

Icing is called when a player on his team's side of the red center line shoots the puck all the way past the red goal line aside from the goal. It is a violation when teams are at equal strength or on the power play. Play is halted when icing is called. The puck is returned to the opposite end of the ice for a faceoff in the offending team's zone.

There are several scenarios in which icing is not called. Among them is when the goaltender leaves the crease to play the puck even it remains untouched. The official might also rule that an opposing player did not make a strong enough attempt to stop the puck from crossing the red goal line or if it was deemed to be an attempted pass rather than a bid to clear the puck to the other end.

Offsides is called when the attacker reaches the defending team's blue line before the puck. The purpose of offsides is to prevent players from cherry-picking up the ice as occurs when a basketball player leaves the defensive end of the court to be all alone on the offensive end in hopes that his teammate will snag a rebound and pass the ball downcourt to him for an easy basket. The blue line in hockey is considered a defender in such cases.

The skate, not the stick, is the determining factor for officials. If both skates are over the blue line before the puck, the player is offsides. If they have only one skate past the blue line and one on it, there is no violation.

QUESTION 43: WHAT MADE "THE GREAT ONE" SO GREAT?

He was the Babe Ruth, the Michael Jordan, the Tom Brady of hockey. He was nicknamed simply "the Great One," but it could have been "the Greatest One." Because Wayne Gretzky is considered by hockey fans and experts as the finest NHL player to ever lace up a pair of skates.

The numbers alone are astonishing. During his twenty-one-year career, mostly with the Edmonton Oilers and Los Angeles Kings, he scored a ridiculous 2,857 points on 894 goals and 1,963 assists. That is not merely an all-time record. It is a mark that will likely never be broken. Gretzky remained through 2022 more than 1,000 points ahead of Jaromir Jagr, who in 2016 bypassed Mark Messier for second place on the all-time list.

Imagine such statistical dominance in other sports. It would be akin to a slugger in baseball smashing 1,097 career home runs—335 more than current record holder Barry Bonds. Or an NBA player scoring 55,205 points—16,868 more than the 38,337 tallied by Kareem Abdul-Jabbar (who held the record until February 2023). Gretzky compiled a staggering average of 1.92 points per game. Pittsburgh Penguins superstar Mario Lemieux finished his career close behind but played five hundred fewer games, eliminating him from the comparison conversation.

The result was that Gretzky owned the Hart Trophy as NHL Most Valuable Player during his peak. He earned it every year from 1980 to 1987 while leading the league in points in each of those seasons. He paced the NHL in goals five times but was particularly adept at passing the puck. He finished atop the assist list an amazing thirteen years in a row.

So, what made Gretzky so special? He considered it instinct, a knack for anticipating puck placement and where a play would take him. He was a hockey savant with incredible athleticism. But though he learned along the way, he was right that much of his greatness was inborn. He had been cited as the next hockey superstar by age nine. Gretzky also had the motivation. He wanted to break all the records set by his hockey hero Gordie Howe. Mission accomplished.

Gretzky performed with seeming effortlessness, spinning to avoid defenders with balletic grace and precision to deliver pinpoint passes to teammates for scores, or slamming the puck into the net himself. His ice vision was unparalleled. He was as close to the perfect athlete as ever competed in major North American sports.

But his greatness would certainly have been diminished had he not risen to the occasion time and again in the postseason. Gretzky averaged 1.84 points per game against premier playoff competition. That was no small feat given the strain of playing for two-and-a-half months to win a Stanley Cup. He is the leading playoff scorer in NHL history and holds the record for the most game-winning goals in the postseason. His brilliance played a critical role in the Oilers winning four crowns in five years from 1984 to 1988.

The Great One earned his nickname. Though such names as Bobby Orr and Gordie Howe are sometimes cited when discussions arise about the finest player to ever grace NHL ice, Gretzky is mentioned most often. What is not debatable is that he was the most explosive offensive force ever.

QUESTION 44: WHICH NHL FRANCHISES HAVE DOMINATED IN THE TWENTY-FIRST CENTURY?

The answer is none to the extent that the Montreal Canadiens dominated the sport through much of their history. But several franchises have achieved tremendous success since the turn of the century. And the short list makes it obvious that the NHL has flipped the script over the years. Neither the Canadiens nor the Toronto Maple Leafs, who have combined for thirty-seven Stanley Cup crowns, won one from 1994 to 2022.

The Chicago Blackhawks was the lone old-school team to snag three or more crowns in the 2000s. The others were the Pittsburgh Penguins (born in the Great Expansion year of 1967) and Tampa Bay Lightning, who expanded into existence in 1992.

Chicago managed to take three championships from 1927 to 2009. But the Blackhawks found their groove thereafter and earned three more over the next six years behind new coach Joel Quenneville. They sported winning records for ten consecutive seasons and captured the Stanley Cup in 2010, 2013, and 2015 with brilliant right wing Patrick Kane leading the way. They finished with a tremendous 35–7 record in the lockout-shortened 2012–2013 season.

They boasted well-balanced clubs. The Blackhawks placed third in goals scored and fifth in goals-against in 2010, and second and first in those two categories, respectively, in 2013. Though they struggled a bit offensively in 2015, their defense made up for it by holding opponents to the lowest scoring total in the NHL behind goaltender Corey Crawford.

The Penguins rode the explosive center duo of wunderkind Sidney Crosby and twenty-two-year-old Russian import Evgeni Malkin to the 2009 crown, their first since Mario Lemieux terrorized foes in the early 1990s. Crosby the Malkin combined to 216 points to lead the team into the playoffs, which the team showed pluck beyond their years by winning a Game 7 against the Philadelphia Flyers to advance into the second round and another against the Detroit Red Wings to take home the title.

Malkin remained a force on the ice when he played, but his impact faded due to injury. Injuries also cost Crosby most of the seasons from 2011 to 2013, but he returned to full-time duty healthy and with a vengeance and led his team to two more championships. He paced the Penguins in points scored and to the titles in 2016 and 2017.

The newest team to forge a mini dynasty was the Lightning, who captured crowns in 2004, 2020, and 2021. Russian-born right wing Nikita Kucherov, who had led the league in assists and points scored in 2019 in winning the Hart Trophy paced the attack during the first of those championship seasons but the team those years thrived mostly on offensive balance. The Lightning were so dominant during the 2020 and 2021 playoffs that they were extended to seven games only once in seven series.

Parity is a goal of all major sports leagues. Dynasties such as those crafted by the Canadiens in hockey, Boston Celtics in basketball, and New York Yankees in baseball often provide an increased level of fan interest. But having more teams in contention consistently creates more attention among more fans for longer periods of time during the regular season and playoffs. The NHL has achieved strong balance after Wayne Gretzky and his Edmonton Oilers enjoyed their reign of terror in the 1980s. No team won more than two Stanley Cups in a row from that time through 2022.

QUESTION 45: WHEN HAVE NHL PLAYERS COMPETED IN THE OLYMPICS?

The Miracle on Ice earned its title after a group of college players defeated the mighty Russian National Team. Had Americans competing in the NHL beaten the Soviets and gone on to win the gold medal, few would have blinked an eye.

Professional athletes were disallowed from competition until the International Olympic Committee opened it up to them in 1986. But the NHL did not always take advantage of the opportunity. Scheduling issues and a lack of desire to interrupt its season led to decisions to prevent its players from competing in the Games. Halting the season for two weeks so its top talent could participate in the Olympics was considered unpalatable to all involved, particularly fans of the teams that lost them with stronger allegiances to their NHL favorites.

The league believed rightly that they had little to gain but much to lose in the eyes of the world by sending its best to the Olympics. The US and Canadian teams featuring premier NHL players were expected by many to take silver and gold. They would receive little credit if they did. But if they did not they were deemed a huge disappointment.

The problem was that Eastern European countries such as the Soviet Union before it dissolved trained its athletes as full-time amateurs. They received training in sports such as hockey with the same zeal as professionals. They might have been students or soldiers, but they were working on maximizing their skills full-time. The result was Russian dominance in Olympic hockey before and after 1980.

Opening up the Games to NHL talent evened the playing field. Those who joined the league out of Europe could still compete for their native countries. But the huge advantage to the International Olympic Committee (IOC) decision belonged to Canada. That nation produced the largest number of top NHL players.

One outcome was predictable from the start. Amateur players in both Canada and the United States expressed disappointment that their dreams of participating in the Olympics had been quashed. But the Canadians did not dominate from the start, despite an outrageous roster that included goaltenders Patrick Roy and Martin Brodeur, defenseman Ray Bourque, and super scorers Wayne Gretzky and Eric Lindros. They proved quite disappointing in the 1998 Games in Japan, falling to superb goalie Dominik Hasek and Czechoslovakia in the semifinal game and failing to medal.

A US team boasting such NHL talent as the league's leading scorer Keith Tkachuk, as well as Chris Chelios and Brett Hull, performed far worse on and off the ice. The Americans were not only eliminated in the quarterfinals by the Czechs after scoring a mere nine goals in four games, but they trashed their rooms in the Olympic Village after elimination, causing about $1,000 in damages.

The United States learned from its mistakes and played much better in 2002, with Hull and Chelios returning and Hall of Fame defenseman Brian Leetch still playing at a high level. The team dominated early in the competition, burying Finland, Belarus, and Germany by a combined score of 19–1, then edging Russia. But the Canadians featuring such NHL offensive talent as Joe Sakic, Mario Lemieux, and Steve Yzerman, as well as Brodeur in goal, proved too strong in the gold-medal game. That the two teams played for all the marbles gave the league something to crow about on an international level after a disappointing showing in 1998.

The two teams returned to the dumper four years later. Canada tried to put together a more balanced roster but failed to include the offensive firepower that defined its previous groups. The

Canadians barely survived the preliminaries, getting blanked by lowly Switzerland and eventual silver-medalist Finland along the way. Yet another shutout against Russia knocked them out in the quarterfinals. Nearly $100 million in NHL talent had failed.

"Nobody could make me feel any worse than I feel right now," said Team Canada coach Pat Quinn after the final defeat. "We had great expectations for ourselves and we didn't meet them. We just weren't as good a team as we needed to be to advance."[94]

Their NHL counterparts playing for the United States suffered a similar fate—only a bit worse. The US team also struggled to score. Their five forwards failed to tally any goals throughout the 2006 Games, leading to consecutive losses to Slovakia, Sweden, and Russia. The team played better with their survival at stake, but a 4–3 defeat against the Finns sent the players packing.

The on-again, off-again fates of the United States and host Canada continued in 2010 as both met again for gold. The United States opened the event by avenging its 2006 defeat to Switzerland, then continued its run by burying Norway and even knocking off its NHL brethren up north. A defeat of Switzerland and stunningly lopsided victory over Finland placed the Americans in the finals.

The city of Vancouver and the entire Canadian nation was revved up for the battle before a sellout crowd. It proved to be a classic. Team Canada appeared destined to roll to victory after taking a 2–0 lead late in the second period. But a deflected pass that scooted past goaltender Roberto Luongo via Ryan Kesler gave the US team a goal and hope heading into the third.

That is when US goaltender Ryan Miller played hero. He saved shot after blistering shot to keep his team alive. Miller and his defensive mates were eventually rewarded when Zach Parise rebounded one past Luongo to tie the game and send it into overtime. Soon Pittsburgh Penguins superstar Sidney Crosby was slamming the puck past Miller for gold.

"That was a game for the ages," said Toews. "It doesn't get any better than that. I'm sure it'll be very memorable for a lot of people and especially for the guys in that locker room that found a way to win."[95]

The Olympic roller-coaster ride continued for the United States in 2014. A US team featuring thirteen of the same players from four years earlier played well early in the tournament before losing to Canada 1–0 in the semifinals. A 5–0 defeat to Finland in the bronze medal game turned their overall performance from promising to disappointing.

There was no disgrace falling again to the Canadians, who had constructed perhaps their finest Olympic roster. They allowed just three goals in six games and dominated Sweden, 3–0, to snag another gold medal. It was the lowest goal count scored against any gold medalist since 1928.

Hockey fans who yearned to continue to follow the Olympic journeys of NHL players were sorely disappointed when the league announced in 2017 that they would not participate the following winter. League commissioner Gary Bettman claimed that the seventeen-day break interrupting the regular season was no longer palatable.

"I think the realities of Olympic participation are more apparent to our Board now and I think it just leads to less enthusiasm about the disruption," offered deputy commissioner Bill Daly. "Quite frankly we don't see what the benefit is from the game standpoint or the league standpoint with respect to Olympic participation."[96]

The same held true in 2022. All that was left was memories. But there were some fond ones for NHL players who had experienced the Olympic dream.

QUESTION 46: WHO WAS THE ONLY JAPANESE-BORN NHL PLAYER?

Yutaka Fukufuji did not play long or particularly well when asked upon to step into goal for the third period of a game for the Los Angeles Kings on January 13, 2007. But it remained, through 2022, a historic moment in league history. Fukufuji remained from that point forward the only Japanese-born player to suit up for an NHL game.

He was pressed into action for the struggling Barry Brust, who had allowed five goals in two periods to the St. Louis Blues. Emotions swept over the twenty-four-year-old Fukufuji. "I was so nervous but I was excited too," he said.[97]

Fukufuji was not too nervous to stop the first shot to come his way. He made a tough save on a Doug Weight slap shot but seconds later surrendered a Dennis Wideman power-play goal that all but clinched a Kings defeat.

That was one of only four NHL games in which Fukufuji participated, all of which were in defeat, as he saved just thirty-six of forty-three shots peppered in his direction. But the statistics proved more meaningless every year that went by without another Japanese player in the league.

Fukufuji launched his career with the Kokudo Rabbits of the Asia League. He caught the eye of Kings scout Glen Williamson and was selected in the eighth round of the 2004 draft. He was the first Asian player taken since Hiroyuki Miura by the Montreal Canadiens in 1992. Miura never played in an NHL game.

The Cincinnati Cyclones of the mid-level East Coast Hockey League proved to be a fine launching pad for Fukufuji. He played particularly well for the Bakersfield Condors of that same league during the 2004–2005 season when he led the team in wins (27), goals-against average (2.48), and shutouts (3).

His mid-December 2006 promotion to the Kings resulted in press conferences on both sides of the Pacific. But he was overwhelmed by the competition. Three days after allowing the game-winner to St. Louis, he was pulled after giving up three goals on nine shots to the Atlanta Thrashers. He was sent back to the Condors after the 2007–2008 season and never again earned a spot on an NHL team. He played for the Netherlands in 2009 and then returned to play in Japan in 2010. His talents helped that country earn a silver medal in the 2011 Asian Games.

His short stint in the NHL did not give hockey traction in Japan as a popular sport. Japanese hockey officials have hoped that a standout might emerge who would help the game gain far more popularity. "It would be huge for the development of the game here," Fukufuji said. Former NHL center Mike Kennedy, who went on to coach the Yokohama Grits of the Asia League, suggested that young Japanese players required more experience on the ice. "We have to take the best kids when they are young and compress the time [they have puck possession]," he said. "Put them in situations where they are in struggle mode, so they don't just go out and skate around, get then to think about solving problems. And when you do that more often the whole level in Japan will go up."[98]

The game took off on local levels in Japan. The International Ice Hockey Federation reported 7,656 male and 1,439 female registered players in the country in 2021, as well as 9,546 junior players. And whereas the sport's popularity was once centered on the northernmost island of Hokkaido, it eventually spread to more populous regions near Tokyo. Japan boasted five professional teams in the Asia League, including one in Yokohama, which boasts a population of nearly four million.

Any success within Japan did not translate into Olympic men's hockey. The national team often failed to qualify for the Winter Games and finished no higher than eighth in eight attempts when it did. But the women's team fared better. They performed particularly well in 2022, beating Sweden, Denmark, and the Czech Republic to qualify for the playoff round before falling to eventual bronze medalist Finland.

Many hope that future achievements on the international level will increase the popularity of hockey in Japan. Even one great talent that makes an impact in the NHL could also do the trick. "Hockey is still a minor sport here in Japan," Kennedy said. "But there is a superstar out there somewhere coming up."[99]

QUESTION 47: HOW DID BUFFALO GOALTENDER TOM BARRASSO MAKE HISTORY?

No NHL player, let alone a goaltender, ever experienced a speedier rise to greatness than Tom Barrasso.

Barrasso spent the 1982–1983 season playing for Acton-Boxborough High School in Massachusetts. His team played twenty-three games without a defeat, mostly because of his goals-against average of 0.99. His brilliance motivated the Buffalo Sabres to select him fifth overall in the first round of the draft.

Similar scenarios had played out with others in hockey history. But Barrasso was about to take the notion of meteoric rise to another level. His talent inspired the Sabres to peg him as their starting goalie that fall. He lost just twice in his first fourteen games as an eighteen-year-old and held the opposition under four goals in eleven of them.

Barrasso continued to perform well enough to earn the Calder Memorial Trophy as Rookie of the Year and even the Vezina Trophy as top NHL goaltender while earning a spot on the all-star team.

Given the start to his career, one might assume he was eventually enshrined into the Hockey Hall of Fame. But after a fine second season in which he led the league in goals-against average, he never performed at the same level. Barrasso did enjoy a fine and long career, mostly as a starter with Buffalo and Pittsburgh before finishing with St. Louis in 2003. His butterfly style of goaltending and positioning were greatly admired, but he also gained a reputation for vulnerability against on-ice shots near the post and allowing long-range shots to get through for goals.

QUESTION 48: WHO IS PATRICK MARLEAU AND WHOSE RECORD DID HE BREAK?

There are those that believe that some records are *not* meant to be broken. The logic is that they are held by such legends that they should belong to them forever.

Among such marks reflect longevity. And the name that was synonymous with that admirable achievement was Gordie Howe, who played in 1,767 games during two separate stints in the NHL from 1946 to 1980. The fact that he also competed in 419 games in the World Hockey Association with sons Mark and Marty and did not retire until age fifty-two made that accomplishment even more remarkable.

So, when a far inferior talent—as were nearly all who have played the sport—broke his all-time record on April 20, 2021, some scoffed. Others were happy for Patrick Marleau, who was considered such a positive person on and off the ice that he received annual votes for the sportsmanship-inspired Lady Byng Trophy.

Marleau broke in with San Jose in 1997 and remained a fixture with that perennial playoff disappointment before a brief fling with the Toronto Maple Leafs starting in 2018 and a return to the Sharks two years later. Nobody can last as long as he did in the league without production, and he was no exception. But despite consistent scoring that peaked at eighty-six in 2006, the center never earned an all-star nod.

And that raised the following question: Should Marleau be voted into the Hockey Hall of Fame based greatly on performing well enough to remain on the ice for a third decade of the twenty-first century?

Arguments for and against have been waged. Though his teams never won a Stanley Cup championship, one can never heap blame on one player in a team sport, particularly one such as Marleau, who performed well and with grit throughout his career. He hung up his skates with 566 goals and 1,197 assists during the regular season and 127 points in the playoffs. Some in the Hall of Fame proved less prolific.

Marleau was also consistent. He scored at least twenty-one goals on fifteen occasions from 1998 forward and thirty goals or more in seven seasons. He played in an era in which obstruction was not merely allowed but encouraged. Had he played in an era during which NHL rules favored scoring, he undoubtedly would have put the puck into the net more often.

It must also be cited that the Hockey Hall of Fame accepts those who perform well on the international stage as well. Marleau earned an International Ice Hockey Federation gold medal in 2003 and was a two-time gold medalist for Canada in 2010 and 2014. He contributed seven assists and two goals to those Olympic efforts, though it helped that the helpers were achieved playing alongside the best in the sport.

Those who contend that Marleau did not earn Hall of Fame status point out his yearly averages. He never finished higher than eighth in Hart Trophy voting for Most Valuable Player and rarely received much consideration for any other awards aside from the Selke Trophy as the top defensive forward. He only earned votes for an award aside from the Lady Byng Trophy seven times.

Marleau was a very good player for a long time. But following his retirement in 2021, only time would tell whether the distinction of having played in the most NHL games ever would earn him induction into the Hockey Hall of Fame.

QUESTION 49: WHY WAS AN NHL GAME IN 1988 CALLED "FOWL"?

Detroit Red Wings fans were known for throwing octopuses on the ice, but somebody at the March 5, 1988, game between in Los Angeles between the Kings and Montreal Canadiens tossed a live chicken into action near the end of the first period. The bird's "playing time" was just over a minute—long enough for it to urinate on the ice.

Indeed, the chicken remained on the ice looking a bit frightened while the action continued before the officials called a halt to the proceedings. He was wearing what appeared to be a cloth napkin in the purple color of the home team. "The chicken was a victim of fowl play," quipped police lieutenant Robert Westlake, who had the perpetrator arrested for malicious mischief and suspicion of cruelty to animals.

The chicken-thrower was thirty-year-old Craig Rodenfels, who had the audacity to ask for the animal back and was refused because it was needed as evidence. He had somehow smuggled the bird into the arena in a sack. It suffered minor bruises and perhaps a bit of emotional trauma as it remained frozen—literally and figuratively—on the ice while hockey players skated around him. The game was eventually stopped, and the chicken was placed in a plastic container.

Media reports speculated that Rodenfels was disgruntled over his team's 4–1 deficit and all-around poor play throughout the season. But no fan had ever expressed disappointment by tossing a chicken onto a playing surface.

"I turned around and there was something on the ice," recalled Kings forward Jim Fox. "I don't know what the heck would be going on; there's not much as far as farming and poultry (in Los Angeles). Hollywood is not known for that."[100]

Other areas of the country certainly are known for farming and poultry. But only once has a live chicken received a bit of playing time in an NHL game.

QUESTION 50: WHO HAD THE BIGGEST IMPACT ON WOMEN'S HOCKEY?

Women's hockey was in its infancy as an international sport when Hayley Wickenheiser joined the Canadian national team in 1993. She eventually earned notoriety as arguably the greatest female player ever.

Wickenheiser was born in 1978 in Shaunavon, Saskatchewan, and excelled in both hockey and softball. She was just fifteen years old when she made her World Championship debut as the youngest player ever to represent Canada in that event. She finished her career having competed in twelve of them and helping her country win seven gold medals. Wickenheiser participated in the first five Olympic Games that included women's hockey and played a key role in Canada winning four of them.

Her achievements included winning tournament Most Valuable Player honors as the leading scorer at the 2002 Games in Salt Lake City with seven goals and three assists. She won those same honors four years later with an even more explosive performance. She tallied five times and added twelve helpers to top all scorers at the Turin Olympics.

Wickenheiser received tremendous recognition at her peak. She won Bobbie Rosenfeld Award in 2007, which is presented annually to the premier Canadian athlete. The honor was well-deserved after she led her team to gold at the World Championships with tournament-best eight goals and six assists.

She had by that time blazed new trails as a female athlete. Playing for Kirkkonummen Salamat in the men's Finnish Elite League in 2003, she became the first women to score a goal in a men's professional league and earned Canadian Athlete of the Year honors. Seven years later she enrolled at the University of Calgary, where she played on the women's hockey team and earned the Broderick Trophy as the Canadian Interuniversity Sport (CIS) Player of the Year. In 2012, she helped that team win its first national championship.

Perhaps her most remarkable achievement that spotlights her athletic versatility was her inclusion on the Canadian softball team in the Sydney Games in 2000. She was the second in that country to earn trips to both the Winter and Summer Olympics, following Bob Boucher (speed stating and track cycling). It came as no surprise when Wickenheiser received the honor as flag bearer for the Canadian team at the 2014 Winter Games in Russia.

Wickenheiser called it quits in 2017 as the leading scorer in the sport internationally. She had racked up 379 points in just 276 international games. Her induction into the Hockey Hall of Fame in 2019 was never in doubt. She remained in the game as assistant director of player development for the Toronto Maple Leafs in 2018 and performed so well in that job that she continued to earn promotions. She was named assistant general manager in 2022, becoming only the fourth woman to land that position on an NHL team.

QUESTION 51: WHO HAD THE FASTEST SLAP SHOT IN NHL HISTORY?

The magazine *Popular Mechanics* caused a bit of a stir in February 1968. It published an article on the science of sport that claimed Chicago Black Hawks perennial all-star and future Hall of Famer Bobby Hull boasted the fastest slap shot in hockey at 118.3 miles per hour. The contention that Hull could rocket the puck faster than anyone was not controversial. But the belief that it reached that speed was greeted with cynicism and has remained highly questionable more than a half-century later.

That is more than ten miles per hour faster than any slap shot recorded since modern technology provide more accurate readings. Moreover, Hull used a wooden stick, which cannot send a puck flying at the same speed as the newer carbon composite variety. And the magazine claim that Montreal Canadiens superstar Jean Beliveau boasted a wrist shot that flew at more than 105 miles an hour caused skepticism about its testing methods and accuracy. It has been offered that *Popular Mechanics* measured the speed of the puck as it left the stick rather than after had traveled twenty feet, which is how it is judged in modern slap shot competitions.

Among those who shots some consider the fastest ever were defensemen, including Nashville Predators and Montreal Canadiens standout Shea Weber, whose blasts were timed at 108.5 miles per hour using a longer stick to compensate for his 6'4" frame. That stick was engineered to store nearly four hundred pounds of force before it broke, almost twice as stiff as more conventional varieties.

Another all-star defenseman noted for his blistering slap shot was Czech import Zdeno Chara, who starred mostly with the Ottawa Senators and Boston Bruins. He used a carbon fiber stick in recording the fastest slapshot in the annual NHL Skills Competition at nearly 106 miles per hour. The 6'9" 250-pound Chara is considered by some as the strongest player in league history, and he used that strength to pepper lightning-fast passes to teammates and shots at the net.

Some players boasted slap shots that gained reputations as the fastest in the sport before they were ever recorded because they passed the eye test. Among them was Hall of Fame Al MacInnis, who starred from 1981 to 2004 with the Calgary Flames and St. Louis Blues. He arrived in the NHL with little more than a booming shot but developed into one of the finest defensemen in league history It came as little surprise when he won seven hardest-shot competitions, more than any other player.

But the fastest of the fast in modern hockey? It might be Al Iafrate, yet another defenseman, whose comparatively mediocre career mostly with Toronto and the Washington Capitals netted just one All-Star Game appearance, though he was beset by injuries that prevented him from maximizing his talent. Iafrate won three of five hardest slapshot battles against MacInnis. He set the record of 105.2 miles per hour with a wooden stick.

The speed at which a player can slam a puck does not equate to the level of effectiveness. Accuracy is more important. It falls more into the category of friendly debate. But such conversations add spice to the sport and help keep NHL talk alive during the offseason.

QUESTION 52: WHO WERE THE FASTEST SKATERS EVER IN THE NHL?

It has been said for good reason that athletes are bigger, stronger, and faster today. Advanced training methods and stronger motivation to maximize athletic qualities for far larger financial rewards are cited as two reasons.

That is certainly true in all sports in which improvement can be confirmed through timings and measurements. Swimming and track and field are two examples. Most people assume it is also true in other sports such as hockey.

The sport requires more quickness than speed—or at least being fast in shorter, rather than longer, bursts both on the offensive and defensive ends. And indeed, players have grown faster and quicker over the years. But that does not mean there weren't speed demons among the earlier greats.

They did not call Maurice Richard "the Rocket" for nothing. He was called "the Cannon" before teammate Ray Getliffe noted that Richard "went in like a rocket" when he attacked the on-scoring opportunities. The local media picked up on the quote and ran with it. Richard's speedskating helped him become the first fifty-goal scorer in NHL history (in just fifty games in 1944) and tally five hundred for a career. His all-around greatness keyed the Montreal Canadiens dynasty of the 1940s and 1950s.

A player who starred a decade later also earned a moniker praising his speed and quickness. And that was Chicago Black Hawks star Bobby Hull. The same *Popular Mechanics* article that clocked the speed of his slap shot claimed "the Golden Jet" reached speeds on the ice of nearly thirty miles per hour.

The 1960s also produced a defenseman considered by many at the time to be the fastest skater ever. Bobby Orr did not revolutionize the defenseman position through force but through scoring and passing accentuated by his gracefulness and speed. Despite the position he played, he often led his Boston teammates down the ice for attacks of the net. Only knee injuries that ended his career at age thirty prevented him from setting records that might have remained intact well into the next century.

The dominant Edmonton Oilers of the 1980s featured several speed demons on the ice but none faster than defenseman Paul Coffey, who performed brilliantly alongside Wayne Gretzky to exceed one hundred points in three consecutive seasons before teaming with Mario Lemieux in Pittsburgh and confirming his Hall of Fame status. He often blurred past unprepared foes to set himself or others up for goals or used his speed to position himself defensively. Coffey was known for his quick acceleration after one or two steps. He finished his career as the top-scoring defenseman in league history.

Richard was not the only NHL "Rocket." Russian Pavel Bure earned the same nickname decades later as a speedy scoring machine with the Vancouver Canucks and Florida Panthers. Defensemen could not match him stride for stride—if they tried to hang by skating next to him, they were invariably beaten. His comparatively slight build and speed reminded some of Yvan Cournoyer, a teammate late in the career of Richard. Bure led the NHL in goals scored three times before knee injuries sapped his speed and cut his Hall of Fame career short.

Right wing Mike Gartner, who played eleven seasons with the Capitals and remained viable with several other teams during his long career, was generally accepted as the fastest skater in the league during his peak well into his thirties. He won the Fastest Skater competition in 1993 and 1996, setting a new record in the second of those events that stood for two decades. His speed and elusiveness allowed him to separate from defenders and create space. His ability to maintain those attributes for well over a decade resulted in thirty-plus goals scored for fifteen consecutive years.

Center Sergei Fedorov, who won the Hart Trophy as league MVP in 1994, helped fuel the glory years of the Detroit Red Wings in the late 1990s and early 2000s. He worked the point on power plays but could use his speed to cover the other end of the ice defensively with his long, powerful strides. Fedorov could not accelerate as quickly as others, but he could fly once he found his momentum. It was no wonder he became the first NHL player to win the "Fastest Skater" contest twice.

The first to take the event three times was Connor McDavid, who through the 2021–2022 season seemed destined for the Hockey Hall of Fame. The Edmonton center led the league in points in four of his first six full seasons. Opponents marveled at his speed, a talent he honed rollerblading in his youth. He was clocked at 25.4 miles per hour, which meant he could get a ticket skating through school zones.

"He glides faster than a lot of us skate," offered Winnipeg Jets forward Mark Scheifele. Even Coffey exclaimed that McDavid "looks like he's in another league" after watching him blow past defenders.[101]

Who was the fastest skater in NHL history? Nobody could ever say for sure. The Fastest Skater competition and knowledge that modern technology and incentive for multimillion-dollar contracts have made all athletes bigger, stronger, and faster can narrow down the field when the topic is debated. But on the other hand, who can claim with certainty that a legend such as Maurice "the Rocket" Richard should not be in the conversation?

QUESTION 53: WHAT WERE THE STRANGEST STANLEY CUP INCIDENTS EVER?

The Stanley Cup is the most iconic trophy in North American sports. One reason is that each player on the winning team is allowed to take it with them for one day and celebrate however he wishes.

That has led to some odd happenings over the years. Such a history of oddities must be presented chronologically.

1905: The Ottawa Senators celebrated their crown with such fervor that one player dropkicked the Cup into a frozen canal.

1924: A group of Canadiens intended to take the Cup with them to a party and enjoy the fruits of their victory when they got a flat tire. They removed the Cup from the trunk to lighten the car, then repaired the tire and went on their merry way. One problem— they left the Cup in the snow. They returned a while later to find it where they left it.

1940: The New York Rangers not only snagged the Stanley Cup in 1940 but also paid off their mortgage at Madison Square Garden. They did what many people do when they pay off a mortgage—they lit it on fire. The difference was that they lit it in the Cup, then put it out by urinating on it. Perhaps that was a bad signal to the hockey gods. The Rangers would not win it again for fifty-four years.

1962: The Toronto Maple Leafs decided to celebrate their championship with a bonfire. They began tossing wood into the flames but mistakenly also pitched the Stanley Cup as well. They got it out but had to pay for the damage.

1964: The Leafs had another boo-boo two years later—or rather a player's son did. Red Kelly was posing for pictures with his little son inside the trophy. When the kid was lifted from the Cup it was discovered that he had left a yellow liquid gift behind.

1993: Pittsburgh Penguins superstar Mario Lemieux decided to take a swim in a pool with the Cup after his team had clinched the crown. But he left it on the bottom of the pool. He should have learned a lesson from Patrick Roy, who had done the same thing two years earlier after the Canadians won it all.

1994: The Rangers teamed up for an unusual celebration after earning their first title since 1940. They took the Cup to nearby Belmont Park and fed Kentucky Derby winner Go for Gin out of it. From one champion to another.

1998: The grossest thing ever done to the Cup came courtesy of Detroit standout Kris Draper. He placed his daughter into the trophy, which seemed like a cute idea until she pooped into it. Unfazed, Draper cleaned it and drank out of it.

2010: Chicago Blackhawks winger Marian Hossa wanted to celebrate winning the Cup by taking it to his native Trencin, Slovakia, where he owned a pierogi factory. He placed a batch of the potato dumplings in the trophy and ate them, then did the same three years later after his team had won another title.

QUESTION 54: WHO WAS SERGEI PRIAKIN, AND HOW DID HE MAKE NHL HISTORY?

The fall of Communism in the Soviet Union and the crumbling of the Eastern Bloc in 1989 had a profound effect on the world. It even led to significant changes in the NHL.

The event opened the league to talent from hockey-rich Eastern Europe. And the first player to arrive was Moscow-born right wing Sergei Priakin, who joined the Calgary Flames late in the 1988–1989 season. He made little impact on the team, scoring three goals and passing for eight assists over two full seasons.

Western European players began competing in the NHL decades earlier. The first was Swedish left wing Ulf Sterner, who donned a New York Rangers uniform for four games in 1965. The first to be drafted was Tommi Salmelainen of Finland, who was selected by the St. Louis Blues in 1969 but never appeared in a game.

The first from across the ocean to star in the league was Swedish defenseman Borje Salming, who landed in the Hockey Hall of Fame after a brilliant career that opened the floodgates for other European standouts. He joined the Maple Leafs in 1973 and earned six consecutive All-Star Game appearances. The Hall of Famer established several franchise records as a fine scorer as well as defender.

Though legendary Black Hawk Stan Mikita was born in Czechoslovakia, he learned the game in North America. The first NHL star born and trained in Eastern Europe was Russian

Alexander Mogilny, who defected to play for the Buffalo Sabres in 1989 and twice exceeded one hundred points in a season. He faded as a scorer after landing in Vancouver but rebounded later in his career to average seventy-three points over three seasons with New Jersey and Toronto.

The flood of European standouts eventually began. By 2022, more than one-quarter of all NHL players were from that continent, including super Russian scorers Alex Ovechkin of the Washington Capitals, who that year passed Gordie Howe as the second-leading goal scorer in league history, and Evgeni Malkin of the Pittsburgh Penguins.

QUESTION 55: WHICH NHL TEAMS TRAVEL THE FARTHEST EVERY YEAR?

The average NHL team travels nearly fifty thousand miles over the course of a regular season. But the players and coaches on some clubs spend far more time flying the friendly skies.

The clear winners are the Edmonton Oilers. Their location in western Canada and lack of proximity to so many cities in the eastern United States forces that team to travel 63,000 miles. That is nearly six thousand miles farther than any other NHL team. Given where Edmonton is located, one might assume the Vancouver Canucks spend the second-most of their frequent flyer miles. That is accurate—they travel nearly 58,000 miles during the season.

Those teams take two of the five longest trips in the league. The Oilers must fly 2,988 miles to play the Florida Panthers. The Canucks are in the air for 3,006 miles before touching down to play the New York Rangers.

Those are not the longest excursions by NHL teams. The Boston Bruins and Seattle Kraken have that distinction. They travel 3,046 miles to compete against each other.

And to think that until the Great Expansion of 1967 there were no franchises in the league west of Chicago in the United States or Toronto in Canada.

QUESTION 56: WHY DOESN'T HOUSTON HAVE AN NHL FRANCHISE?

Every American city that ranks among the top fifteen in population has boasted a franchise in each of the four major sports except one. That one is Houston.

It seems odd to hockey fans that the city that sits behind New York, Los Angeles, and Chicago in population has never had one, particularly given that that league features thirty-two teams. The argument might be that Texas is not a hockey hotbed, but the Dallas Stars have proven to be highly successful both on the ice and at the gate. Those that have advocated for Houston receiving a moved or expansion team cite the interest that would be generated by a rivalry with the Stars.

But Houston spent nearly a decade after losing its minor-league Aeros to Iowa without any professional hockey team. The city did have a team in the World Hockey Association of the same name from 1972 to 1978 but failed to secure an NHL franchise when the league folded. The NHL accepted three Canadian teams and one American one from the WHA. The competition was down to the Aeros and Hartford Whalers. The latter was chosen despite a huge discrepancy in city populations and the proximity of Hartford to Boston, where the Bruins were king. Houston therefore became the only WHA champion to not land in the NHL.

Aeros owner Kenneth Schnitzer turned his attention to acquiring an NHL franchise through relocation. He set his sights on the struggling Cleveland Barons and came close to making a deal before the club was purchased by the owner of the Minnesota North Stars. Schnitzer was forced to disband the franchise in 1979.

Another Aeros iteration joined the International Hockey League as an expansion team in 1994 and merged into the American Hockey League eight years later when the IHL folded. Further attempts had been made to find an NHL team that sought relocation, including the Edmonton Oilers in the 1990s, but every deal fell through.

Houston had proven in the WHA that it could support a major-league team. The Aeros ranked third in league attendance three times during its stint and drew particularly well in winning seasons. The city certainly boasts enough people to draw from with a metropolitan area population of over six million.

The NHL expanded to thirty-two teams with additions in Las Vegas in 2017 and Seattle in 2021. NBA Houston Rockets owner Tillman Fertitta began negotiating with NHL officials to bring a team to his city but spoke about the need to sell at least 14,000 season tickets to make it a viable possibility since league organizations receive far less television revenue than those in the three other major North American sports.

Franchises have come and gone in the NHL—even from cities with large populations such as Atlanta. The league yearns for stability. Expansion beyond thirty-two teams was not considered likely in the third decade of the twenty-first century. Fertitta and anyone else seeking to bring hockey back to Houston at the highest level were therefore forced to wait for an ideal time and circumstance they knew might not arrive for many years.

Notes

1. "History of Hockey–Who Invented Hockey?" Sport Legacy, 2023, http://www.sportlegacy.net/hockey/history-of-hockey.

2. Andrew Forbes, "Who Invented Hockey?" The Hockey Writers, April 26, 2022, https://www.thehockeywriters.com/who-invented-hockey.

3. Ibid.

4. Ibid.

5. "This Week in History: The World's First Organized Hockey Game Was Played on March 3, 1875," McGill University News and Events, March 2, 2012, https://www.mcgill.ca/channels/news/week-history-worlds-first-organized-hockey-game-was-played-march-3-1875-104900.

6. Shawn P. Roarke, "Stanley Cup Has Incredible History."

7. "Facts, Firsts and Faux Paus," Hockey Hall of Fame, https://www.hhof.com/thecollection/stanleycup_factsfirstsfauxpaus.html.

8. "1907 Stanley Cup Championship," Ice Hockey Wiki, https://icehockey.fandom.comwiki/1907_Stanley_Cup_championship.

9. Roarke, "Stanley Cup Has Incredible History," NHL.com, March 13, 2017, https://www.nhl.com/news/stanley-cup-has-incredible-125-years-of-history/c-287633638.

10. Ibid.

11. "History of the Hockey Puck," The Hockey Fanatic, July 11, 2012, https://www.thehockeyfanatic.com/2012/07/history-of-the-hockey-puck/; Ian Palmer, "What Are Hockey Pucks Made of & Who Makes Them?" Brave Stick Hockey, June 1, 2022, https://bshockey.com/hockey-puck-history/#:~:text=Puck%20history.

12. Ibid.

13. Aaron Gordon, "Lame Puck," Slate, January 28, 2014, https://slate.com/culture/2014/01/foxtrax-glowing-puck-was-it-the-worst-blunder-in-tv-sports-history-or-was-it-just-ahead-of-its-time.html.

14. Ibid.

15. Palmer, "What Are Hockey Pucks Made of & Who Makes Them?"

16. Adam Proteau, "From Deaths to Monsters, a History of Fighting in Hockey," The Hockey News, January 11, 2015, https://thehockeynews.com/news/from-deaths-to-monsters-a-history-of-fighting-in-hockey.

17. Scott Engstrom, "Anatomy of the Hockey Fight: The History, the Purpose, and Current Role of Fighting in the NHL," FanSided, November 12, 2014, https://penslabyrinth.com/2014/11/12/anatomy-of-the-hockey-fight.

18. Proteau, "From Deaths to Monsters, a History of Fighting in Hockey."

19. Greg Wyshynski, "'The New Normal': Why Fighting in the NHL Has Dropped to Historic Lows," ESPN, July 20, 2019, https://www.espn.com/nhl/story/_/id/27283018/the-new-normal-why-fighting-nhl-dropped-historic-lows.

20. Alison Lukan, "Evolution of the Goalie Mask," February 21, 2017, Blue Jackets News, https://www.nhl.com/bluejackets/news/evolution-of-the-hockey-goalie-mask/c-286870424.

21. Dave Stubbs, "Clint Benedict Overshadowed, Not Forgotten," NHL.com, February 20, 2017, https://www.nhl.com/news/clint-benedict-was-one-of-nhls-first-great-goalies/c-286889904.

22. "History of the Goalie Mask," USA Hockey Magazine, 2019, https://www.usahockeymagazine.com/article/history-goalie-mask.

23. "The Evolution of Goalie Masks in Hockey," Goalie Monkey, March 31, 2022, https://www.goaliemonkey.com/learn/hockey-goalie-mask-history.

24. "History of the Goalie Mask.".

25. Ibid.

26. Wayne Jones, "What Percentage of NHL Players Are American?" Hockey Answered, https://hockeyanswered.com/what-percentage-of-nhl-players-are-american.

27. "Which Is the Most Popular Sport in America? Top 5 Revealed," Sports Brief, April 6, 2022, https://sportsbrief.com/facts/14576-discover-popular-sport-america.

28. Mario Tirabassi, "2021 Stanley Cup Final Ratings: Canadian Viewership Set Records, While U.S. Viewers Tuned Out," Bleacher Nation, July 9, 2021, https://www.bleachernation.com/blackhawks/2021/07/09/2021-stanley-cup-final-tv-ratings-canadian-viewership-set-records-while-u-s-viewers-tuned-out.

29. Brian McFarlane, "Early Leagues and the Birth of the NHL," WashingtonCaps.com, https://capitals.ice.nhl.com/club/page.htm?bcid=his_EarlyLeagues.

30. Associated Press, "'Great Expansion' of 1967 Showed NHL Was for Real," Northwest Arkansas Democrat Gazette, February 11, 2016, https://www.nwaonline.com/news/2016/feb/11/great-expansion-of-1967-showed-nhl-was-.

31. Susan Ormiston, "Russian Classic Marks 50 years of Canada-Russia Hockey Rivalry with 1966 Match Redux," CBC, February 11, 2016, https://www.cbc.ca/news/world/hockey-russia-sherbrooke-beavers-1.3440326.

32. Rick Maese, "So They Meet Again: U.S., Canada Again Face Off for Women's Hockey Gold," Washington Post, February 20, 2018, https://www.washingtonpost.com/sports/olympics/so-they-meet-again-us-canada-again-face-off-for-womens-hockey-gold/2018/02/20/b625bf66-1603-11e8-b681-2d4d462a1921_story.html.

33. Staff writer, "Franchise Firsts: Damian Rhodes Scores a Goal," NHL.com, November 2, 2012, https://www.nhl.com/senators/news/franchise-firsts-damian-rhodes-scores-a-goal/c-644814.

34. Shaun Smith and Bryan Bastin, "A Brief History of Goalie Goals," SB Nation, January 10, 2020, https://www.ontheforecheck.com/2020/1/10/21059616/a-brief-history-of-goalie-goals-nhl-pekka-rinne-scores-against-chicago.

35. Jamie Bradburn, "Toronto Invents: The Hat Trick," Torontoist, April 3, 2013, https://torontoist.com/2013/04/toronto-invents-the-hat-trick.

36. Ibid.

37. Devan McGuinness, "What Happens to the Hats Thrown on the Ice after a Hat Trick in Hockey?" Distractify, November 9, 2021, https://www.distractify.com/p/what-happens-to-the-hats-thrown-on-the-ice-after-a-hat-trick.

38. Matthew Zator, "NHL Hat Tricks History and Fun," The Hockey Writers, December 12, 2022, https://thehockeywriters.com/nhl-hat-tricks-history-fun-facts.

39. "Peter S. Cusimano Obituary," Detroit News, https://www.legacy.com/us/obituaries/detroitnews/name/peter-cusimano-obituary?id=12325031.

40. Kirkland Crawford, "Detroit Red Wings' Octopus-Throwing Tradition: Where'd It Come From?" Detroit Free Press, June 14, 2018, https://www.freep.com/story/sports/nhl/red-wings/2018/06/14/detroit-red-wings-octopus-throwing-tradition/703148002.

41. Frank Ahrens, "The Octopus on the Ice," Washington Post, June 11, 1998, https://www.washingtonpost.com/archive/lifestyle/1998/06/11/the-octopus-on-the-ice/d7383c03-27e4-4820-bccb-8df6858a6715.

42. Ibid.

43. PETA, "PETA to Red Wings: Toss Octopus-Tossing Fans Out of Joe Louis Arena," PETA, April 7, 2017, https://www.peta.org/blog/peta-asks-detroit-red-wings-ban-octopus-throw.

44. George Sipple, "Red Wings: Man Not Banned for Hurling Octopus in Little Caesars Arena," *Detroit Free Press*, October 11, 2017, https://www.freep.com/story/sports/nhl/red-wings/2017/10 /11/detroit-red-wings-octopus-ban/755059001.

45. "What Is a Face-Off in Hockey?" Stadium Reviews, December 3, 2021, https://thestadiumreviews.com/blogs/info /what-is-a-face-off-in-hockey.

46. Ibid.

47. Tab Bamford, "Odd Man Rush," The Fourth Period, https:// www.thefourthperiod.com/odd-man-rush.

48. Brandon Storey, "What Is a Rush in Ice Hockey?" Hockey Questions, https://hockeyquestion.com/what-is-rush-hockey.

49. "Hockey 101: NHL vs. Olympic Game Changers," NBC Olympics, February 14, 2022, https://www.nbcolympics.com/news /hockey-101-nhl-vs-olympic-game-changers.

50. "How Thick Is the Ice in a Hockey Rink?" FloHockey, May 1, 2022, https://www.flohockey.tv/articles/7971572-how-thick -is-the-ice-in-a-hockey-rink.

51. Ibid.

52. Chris Peters, "Inside the Miracle on Ice: How Team USA Defied the Numbers to Beat the Soviet Union at the 1980 Olympics," ESPN, February 19, 2020, https://www.espn.com/nhl/story/_/id /28701139/inside-miracle-ice-how-team-usa-defied-numbers -beat-soviet-union-1980-olympics.

53. Jane Rogers, "Do You Believe in Miracles (on Ice)?" National Museum of American History, February 21, 2014, https:// americanhistory.si.edu/blog/2014/02/do-you-believe-in-miracles -on-ice.html.

54. Peters, "Inside the Miracle on Ice: How Team USA Defied the Numbers to Beat the Soviet Union at the 1980 Olympics."

55. Ibid.

56. Ibid.

57. Callum Borchers and Chris Citorik, "Mike Eruzione Reflects on the 'Miracle on Ice,' 40 Years Later," Radio Boston, February 21, 2020, https://www.wbur.org/radioboston/2020/02/21/miracle-40-ice-hockey-olympics-eruzione.

58. Wayne Jones, "How Do Hockey Players Know When to Change?" Hockey Answered, https://hockeyanswered.com/how-do-hockey-players-know-when-to-change/#:~:text=Hockey%20players%20know%20when%20to%20change%20based%20on%20a%20number,cause%20a%20scoring%20chance%20against.

59. Wayne Jones, "How Many Calories Does a Hockey Player Burn?" Hockey Answered, https://hockeyanswered.wpengine.com/how-many-calories-does-a-hockey-player-burn-nhl-recreation.

60. Jones, "How Do Hockey Players Know When to Change?"

61. "How Do Players Know When to Change Lines?" Brave Stick Hockey, June 1, 2022, https://bshockey.com/how-do-hockey-players-know-when-to-change-lines.

62. Jones, "How Do Hockey Players Know When to Change?"

63. "Inside the Dressing Room," NHL.com, August 30, 2006, https://www.nhl.com/canadiens/news/inside-the-dressing-room/c-489201.

64. John McCrae, "In Flanders Fields," Poetry Foundation, https://www.poetryfoundation.org/poems/47380/in-flanders-fields.

65. Arpon Basu, "Where the Ghosts Live: How the Canadiens Dressing Room Evolved and How the Dynamics of That Room Work," The Athletic, February 18, 2019, https://theathletic.com/818758/2019/02/18/where-the-ghosts-live-how-the-canadiens-dressing-room-evolved-and-how-the-dynamics-of-that-room-work.

66. "Hockey 101: The Ice Hockey Rink," The Hockey Writers, January 26, 2014, https://thehockeywriters.com/hockey-101-ice-hockey-rink/#:~:text=Lines%20on%20the%20Hockey%20

Rink&text=Two%20thick%20blue%20lines%20cross,both%20 ends%20of%20the%20rink.

67. Jason Diamos, "Brodeur Feels Defanged by NHL's New Rule," *New York Times*, September 16, 2005, https://www.ny times.com/2005/09/16/sports/hockey/brodeur-feels-defanged -by-nhls-new-rule.html.

68. Ibid.

69. "Brodeur's Legacy: The Trapezoid Rule," Scouting the Refs, February 9, 2016, https://scoutingtherefs.com/2016/02 /11917/brodeurs-legacy-the-trapezoid-rule.

70. Ibid.

71. "Tommy 'Cowboy' Anderson 1936 New York Americans," Hockey Gods, https://hockeygods.com/images/19908-Tommy __Cowboy__Anderson_1936_New_York_Americans #:~:text=Anderson%20won%20the%201942%20Hart,to%20 follow%20suit%20in%201954.

72. "Two Line Pass Rule: How the NHL Removing It Changed Hockey," Hockey Monkey, April 4, 2022, https://www.hockey monkey.com/learn/2-line-pass#:~:text=The%20two%2Dline%20 pass%20rule,red%20line%20during%20the%20pass.

73. Brendan Azoff, "Good Defense Will Defeat Good Offense in NHL Playoffs," Hockey Writers, August 9, 2020, https://the hockeywriters.com/nhl-defense-wins-stanley-cups.

74. Sean McIndoe, "Why Were the '80s So Insane in the NHL?" Grantland, August 27, 2014, https://grantland.com/the -triangle/why-were-the-80s-so-insane-in-the-nhl.

75. "The Evolution of Europeans in the NHL," The Hockey Writers, May 12, 2022, https://thehockeywriters.com/the -evolution-of-europeans-in-the-nhl.

76. Zach Pekale, "Colleges with the Most NHL 1st-Round Draft Picks, All Time," NCAA: Men's Hockey, July 26, 2021, https://www.ncaa.com/news/icehockey-men/article/2021-07-26 /colleges-most-nhl-1st-round-draft-picks-all-time.

77. Daniel Harris, "The Forgotten Story of Great Britain's Gold at the 1936 Winter Games," Eurosport, February 2, 2018, https://www.eurosport.com/ice-hockey/fascism-and-gb-s-ice-hockey-gold-in-1936_sto6499246/story.shtml.

78. "IHLC Results–Great Britain 2-1 Canada–11 Feb 1936," International Hockey Lineal Championship, https://theihlc.com/1936/02/11/ihlc-results-great-britain-2-1-canada-feb-11-1936.

79. "A Brief History of the Zamboni," *The Week*, January 8, 2015, https://theweek.com/articles/441560/brief-history-zamboni#:~:text=Who%20invented%20the%20Zamboni%3F,used%20his%20family%20name%20instead.

80. Facts Verse, "Why Jay Thomas Was Killed Off Cheers," YouTube video, March 2, 2021, https://www.youtube.com/watch?v=7c7ZExsc1kM&ab_channel=FactsVerse.

81. Stu Hackel, "Why I Hate the Shootout," SI.com, December 8, 2010, https://www.si.com/nhl/2010/12/08/for-better-or-worse-shootouts-here-to-stay.

82. Larry Schwartz, "Orr Brought More Offense to Defense," ESPN, https://www.espn.com/sportscentury/features/00016391.html#:~:text=Bobby%20Orr%20is%20the%20only,What%20a%20revolutionary%20concept.

83. Ibid.

84. Dave Stubbs, "McDonald Played Vital Role in Shaping Orr's Career," NHL.com, July 21, 2022, https://www.nhl.com/web/news/bucko-mcdonald-vital-role-in-bobby-orrs-career/c-335037036.

85. Ryan Dixon, "Greatest Hate of All," Sportsnet, https://www.sportsnet.ca/hockey/nhl/habs-vs-bruins-the-greatest-hate-of-all.

86. "Explaining the Unwritten Rules and Etiquette of a Hockey Fight," NBC Sports Washington, January 30, 2019, https://www.nbcsports.com/washington/capitals/explaining-unwritten-rules-and-etiquette-hockey-fight.

87. "Stop the Blog–The Butterfly," STP Goaltending, April 12, 2019, https://stpgoaltending.com/stop-the-blog/f/stop-the-blog---the-butterfly.

88. Ken Campbell, "Tony Esposito: The Quiet Trailblazer," Hockey Unfiltered, August 11, 2021, https://kencampbell.substack.com/p/tony-esposito-the-quiet-trailblazer.

89. Associated Press, "Players Want NHL to Increase Diversity, Anti-Racism Efforts," ESPN, October 6, 2022, https://www.espn.com/nhl/story/_/id/34738789/players-want-nhl-increase-diversity-anti-racism-efforts.

90. Stephen Whyno, "'A Movement Is Not a Moment': NHL Focuses on Racial Diversity," *Amsterdam News*, June 23, 2022, https://amsterdamnews.com/news/2022/06/23/a-movement-not-a-moment-nhl-focuses-on-racial-diversity.

91. Ibid.

92. Akim Aliu, "Hockey Is Not for Everyone," *The Players' Tribune*, May 19, 2020, https://www.theplayerstribune.com/articles/hockey-is-not-for-everyone-akim-aliu-nhl.

93. Terrence Doyle, "The NHL Says, 'Hockey Is for Everyone.' Black Players Are Not So Sure." FiveThirtyEight, October 19, 2020, https://fivethirtyeight.com/features/the-nhl-says-hockey-is-for-everyone-black-players-arent-so-sure.

94. Jonathon Gatehouse, "How It All Went Wrong," *Maclean's*, March 6, 2006, https://archive.macleans.ca/article/2006/3/6/how-it-all-went-wrong.

95. Scott Burnside, "Gold-Medal Battle 'Game for the Ages,'" ESPN, February 28, 2010, https://www.espn.com/olympics/winter/2010/icehockey/columns/story?columnist=burnside_scott&id=4954922.

96. Dan Rosen, "NHL Will Not Participate in 2018 Olympics," NHL.com, April 3, 2017, https://www.nhl.com/news/nhl-will-not-participate-in-2018-winter-olympics/c-288385598.

97. "Fukufuji Becomes First Japanese Player in NHL," NHL.com, January 13, 2007, https://www.nhl.com/news/fukufuji -becomes-first-japanese-player-in-nhl/c-287370.

98. Jim Armstrong, "Trailblazer Yutaka Fukufuji Backstops His Team to Success on Home Ice," Japan Forward, December 18, 2021, https://featured.japan-forward.com/sportslook/ice-hockey -trailblazer-yutaka-fukufuji-backstops-his-team-to-success-on -home-ice.

99. Ibid.

100. "Chicken on the Ice! [March 5, 1988; SC Top 10 Apr. 9, 2012]," YouTube, https://www.youtube.com/watch?v=u2yJ 4lHZjJ0&ab_channel=MikeMatthews.

101. Josh Bell, "12 of the Fastest Skaters Ever in the NHL," The Hockey Writers, December 8, 2022, https://thehockeywriters .com/top-12-fastest-skaters-nhl.